Listed

HUNDREDS OF AMUSING, AMAZING AND DOWNRIGHT WEIRD LISTS.

Published by Carlton Books Limited
20 Mortimer Street
London W1T 3JW

10 9 8 7 6 5 4 3 2 1

Copyright © 2009 Carlton Publishing Group

All rights reserved. This book is sold subject to the condition that it may not be reproduced, stored in a retrieval system or transmitted in any form or by means, electronic, mechanical, photocopying, recording or otherwise, without the publisher's prior consent.

ISBN 978-1-84732-328-6

Printed in China

The text in this book originally appeared in *The Best Book of Lists Ever!*

Listed

HUNDREDS OF AMUSING, AMAZING AND DOWNRIGHT WEIRD LISTS.

CARLTON
BOOKS

INTRODUCTION

Most of us are slaves to lists — whether it be shopping lists, lists of jobs to do, lists of things to take on holiday or lists of places to see when we get there. Only the Leaning Tower of Pisa has a greater list than the average person. And if we're not making lists, we're reading lists compiled by other people — checking the music charts, seeing who's top of the batting averages, flicking through the magazine listings or monitoring our children's education via the school league tables.

Books of lists have been popular since *The Domesday Book*. So why are we so fascinated with them? It is principally because they present information in an easily-digestible format and contain the sort of quirky material not found in standard reference books. This book follows in that noble tradition, offering a wealth of readily-accessible trivia on every major topic under the sun — including sport, the cinema, natural history, music, inventions, television, crime, history, transport, language and geography.

Here you'll find lists to start and end arguments. What better way of passing an evening than to ask your friends to name 20 songs where the title doesn't appear in the lyrics? It's not as easy as it sounds. Or how about ten songs with a fruit in the title? Ten famous people who suffered from piles? Ten celebrities who once had soccer trials? Or, for the true aficionado, ten names for Colonel Mustard in foreign versions of Cluedo?

With more than 140 lists here, it is a book you can dip into any time, anywhere. Keep a copy on the bedside table or in the loo for those quiet moments of meditation. But be warned: you could be locked in there for hours as your thirst for useless knowledge knows no bounds.

Geoff Tibballs.

20 FIRST JOBS OF THE FAMOUS

1. SYLVESTER STALLONE – lion-cage cleaner.
2. WARREN BEATTY – rat-catcher.
3. ERROL FLYNN – sheep-castrator.
4. SEAN CONNERY – French polisher for coffin-maker.
5. CYNDI LAUPER – dog-kennel cleaner.
6. MICK JAGGER – porter at a mental hospital.
7. BETTE MIDLER – pineapple-chunker.
8. ROD STEWART – grave-digger.
9. JEFFREY ARCHER – deckchair attendant.
10. BILL WITHERS – aircraft toilet seat manufacturer.
11. RUSS ABBOTT – hearse driver.
12. MICHAEL DOUGLAS – petrol-pump attendant.
13. JON BON JOVI – Christmas decoration-maker.
14. JACK NICHOLSON – mailing boy.
15. OZZY OSBOURNE – slaughterhouse labourer.
16. ROCK HUDSON – vacuum cleaner salesman.
17. STING – filing clerk with the Inland Revenue.
18. BURT LANCASTER – lingerie salesman.
19. EDITH PIAF – wreath-maker.
20. JOE COCKER – gas fitter.

Warren Beatty's big theatre break came when he was 17 – but it was actually outside the theatre, in the alleyway. The National Theater, Washington DC, had been plagued by rats, one of which had bitten an actor. Equity pressed the management to hire an official rat-catcher and young Beatty, desperate for a job in the theatre, landed that plum role. So while Helen Hayes strode the stage in a revival of *The Skin of Our Teeth*, Beatty patrolled the alley all evening as a rodent deterrent.

> PEOPLE

10 CELEBRITIES WHO ARE SURPRISINGLY SHORT

1. HUMPHREY BOGART 5ft 4in.
2. DAVID BOWIE 5ft 8in.
3. LIAM GALLAGHER 5ft 8in.
4. MEL GIBSON 5ft 8in.
5. JOHN LENNON 5ft 7in.
6. AL PACINO 5ft 6in.
7. ROBERT REDFORD 5ft 8in.
8. FRANK SINATRA 5ft 6in.
9. BRUCE SPRINGSTEEN 5ft 8in.
10. SYLVESTER STALLONE 5ft 7in.

Short men can have big problems on-screen. Alan Ladd (a diminutive 5ft 4in) used to perch on an orange-box or get his leading ladies to stand in a trench so that they could see eye to eye. Similarly when Mel Gibson starred opposite 5ft 11in Sigourney Weaver in *The Year of Living Dangerously*, he had to stand on a box for some scenes. Tom Cruise's PR people insist he is 5ft 9in. But perhaps Daryl Hannah, 5ft 10ins, summed it up when she said: 'I'd love to star in a film with Tom Cruise but I'd have to do the whole movie on my knees.' Some stars accept their lack of stature with dignity. When 5ft 7in Billy Joel married 5ft 10½in Christie Brinkley, he claimed: 'The fact that I can attract such a beautiful woman as Christie should give hope to every short, ugly guy in the world.' Even the 5ft Danny De Vito was philosophical about the description once made of him as being like 'testicles with arms.'

> PEOPLE

10 FAMOUS HYPOCHONDRIACS

1. ADOLF HITLER.
2. KENNETH WILLIAMS.
3. HANS CHRISTIAN ANDERSEN.
4. JOHN KEATS.
5. ARNOLD BENNETT.
6. MARCEL PROUST.
7. NICCOLO PAGANINI.
8. WILLIAM COWPER.
9. DR. SAMUEL JOHNSON.
10. PERCY BYSSHE SHELLEY.

Carry On star Kenneth Williams was obsessed with his bowels. He suffered dreadfully from piles and as a result harboured a deep distrust of other people's lavatories. Whenever he moved into a theatre for a play, he always had his own personal toilet, for his exclusive use. For the same reason, visitors to his London flat were never allowed to use the lavatory there – Williams insisted that they use the public toilets at nearby Tottenham Court Road tube station. Smoking was also forbidden in his flat which was described by one caller as being like a 'spotless, pristine, monk's cell.'

PEOPLE

10 PEOPLE BORN ON CHRISTMAS DAY

1. **SIR ISAAC NEWTON**, scientist (1642).
2. **WILLIAM COLLINS**, poet (1721).
3. **CONRAD HILTON**, hotelier (1887).
4. **DAME REBECCA WEST**, novelist (1892).
5. **CAB CALLOWAY**, jazz singer (1907).
6. **ANWAR SADAT**, statesman (1918).
7. **LITTLE RICHARD**, singer (1935).
8. **KENNY EVERETT**, disc jockey (1944).
9. **ANNIE LENNOX**, singer (1954).
10. **SHANE McGOWAN**, singer (1957).

The most widely-perpetuated myth about Christmas Day births is that Humphrey Bogart was among them. In fact he was born on January 23, 1899 but Warner Bros, sensing publicity possibilities, later changed it to December 25, 1900. Among those who died on Christmas Day were W.C. Fields in 1946 and Charlie Chaplin in 1977. On leaving school in Aberdeen, the only job Annie Lennox could find was at the local Findus fish products factory. The stench was appalling. She remembers: 'I used to wrap my work clothes in a plastic bag each night and fall flat on my face when I opened it the next morning. Working on the plaice-filleting machine made me want to throw up all the time. Yet, looking back, I suppose it was beneficial in discovering exactly what I NEVER wanted to do again.' Moving south, she got a job as a waitress at Pippins restaurant in Hampstead where one of the customers was her future musical partner Dave Stewart.

> PEOPLE

10 POSSIBLE CASES OF SPONTANEOUS HUMAN COMBUSTION

1. On the morning of July 2, 1951 Mrs. Mary Reeser, a 67-year-old widow from St. Petersburg, Florida, was found reduced to ashes in an apartment which showed little sign of damage. The only sign of fire was a small charred area in the middle of the floor in which there were blackened chair springs and Mrs. Reeser's remains. Tremendous heat must have been necessary to incinerate the body, yet only the chair and the table next to it were damaged. The carpet on which the chair stood had not even burned through. Part of the ceiling was coated with soot but a pile of newspapers in the room remained intact. Experts were unable to determine the cause of the fire. Dr. William M. Krogman, a physical anthropologist at the University of Pennsylvania, commented: 'They say truth often is stranger than fiction and this case proves it.'

2. In the summer of 1922 at Sydenham, South London, 68-year-old widow Euphemia Johnson returned home from a shopping trip and made a pot of tea. She carried the hot cup to a table near the window. Later she was discovered fallen from her chair, her body consisting of nothing more than a pile of bones inside clothes which weren't even burnt. The varnish on the chair had bubbled slightly from the heat but the tablecloth was undamaged.

3. On March 1, 1953 at Greenville, South Carolina, Waymon Wood was found 'crisped black' in the front seat of his closed car. Only the windscreen had been affected by the heat and there was half a tank of petrol in the car which hadn't ignited.

4. One evening in the late 1950s, 19-year-old Maybelle Andrews was dancing with her boyfriend Billy Clifford in a London dance-hall when she suddenly burst into flames. The fire raged from her back and chest, enveloping her head and igniting her hair. At the inquest, Billy Clifford said: 'I know it sounds incredible, but it appeared to me that the flames burst outwards, as if they originated within her body.' The verdict was 'death by misadventure, caused by fire of unknown origin.'

PEOPLE

5. At Sowerby Bridge near Halifax in 1899, Sara Kirby found her four-year-old daughter Amy ablaze in her bed. There was no evidence of matches or charred paper. As a distraught Sara went to impart the sad news to her estranged husband who lived nearby, a messenger informed her that her other daughter, five-year-old Alice, had also been found on fire in her bed at her father's house. The two fatal fires had broken out at precisely the same time.

6. On October 9, 1980 Jeanna Winchester, riding in a car in Jacksonville, Florida, suddenly burst into bright yellow flames. Examination of the car revealed little or no fire damage. There was no spilt petrol, the victim wasn't smoking and the car widow was up so nobody could have thrown anything into the vehicle. A fire officer remarked: 'I've never seen anything like it in 12 years in the force.'

7. In 1986 at Essex County, New York, a retired fireman was reduced to a pile of bones and $3\frac{1}{2}$lb of ash following an intense fire. Most of the damage to the house was caused by smoke and the blaze had been so localized that a box of matches, a few feet from his remains, hadn't ignited.

8. In 1943 Madge Knight died in a Chichester hospital after a curious fire at her home. She had been lying in bed when something unknown had set fire to her back. Yet the bedclothes weren't even scorched.

9. Walking along a London street in 1985, a 19-year-old man caught fire from the waist up. He said it was like being doused in burning petrol, yet no traces were found.

10. At Bladeboro, North Carolina, in 1932, a cotton dress being worn by Mrs. Charles Williamson suddenly burst into flames. She was not standing near any fire nor had her dress been in contact with any flammable substance. Over the next few days, a pair of Mr. Williamson's trousers, hanging in the wardrobe, also mysteriously caught fire, followed by a bed and a pair of curtains in an unoccupied room. In each case, the items burned with bluish jet-like flames, yet adjacent objects remained unaffected. Experts were unable to shed any light on the fires.

PEOPLE

10 FAMOUS PEOPLE AND THEIR PETS

1. **LORD BADEN-POWELL** – a hyrax (a small nocturnal mammal) called Hyrie.

2. **CHARLES BAUDELAIRE** – a bat in a cage on his desk.

3. **ROBERT BURNS** – a ewe called Poor Mailie. He wrote two poems about her.

4. **LORD BYRON** – a bear. He kept one at Cambridge University because dogs weren't allowed.

5. **HENRIK IBSEN** – kept a pet scorpion on his desk.

6. **FLORENCE NIGHTINGALE** – kept a small owl in her pocket, even while serving in the Crimean War.

7. **GEORGE ORWELL** – a goat called Muriel.

8. **ROBERT LOUIS STEVENSON** – a donkey called Modestine.

9. **ALFRED, LORD TENNYSON** – a pony named Fanny which used to pull Tennyson's wife in a wheelchair.

10. **VIRGINIA WOOLF** – a marmoset called Mitz.

Edward Lear kept a striped tomcat called Foss, a creature with a curious stub tail. In 1881, Lear had to move to a new house in Italy because the building of a hotel blocked the view and ruined the light for Lear's painting. To make sure that Foss felt at home, Lear had his new house, the Villa Tennyson, built as an exact replica of their previous abode. Distinguished actor Sir Ralph Richardson used to ride his motorcycle to the theatre even when in his seventies, sometimes arriving with his pet parrot, José, on his left shoulder. He also kept a ferret called Eddie and, to the horror of his leading ladies, would often secrete a white mouse in his pocket.

> PEOPLE

10 CELEBRITIES WITH RED INDIAN BLOOD

1. CHER (Armenian, Turkish, French, Cherokee).

2. JOHNNY DEPP (part-Cherokee – has tattoo of Cherokee Indian Chief).

3. FARRAH FAWCETT (French, English, $1/8$ Choctaw Indian).

4. SALLY FIELD (part-Cherokee).

5. JAMES GARNER (part-Cherokee).

6. WAYLON JENNINGS (part-Cherokee, part-Comanche).

7. DOLLY PARTON (Dutch, Irish and Cherokee).

8. BURT REYNOLDS (Italian and Cherokee).

9. ROY ROGERS (part-Choctaw).

10. DENNIS WEAVER (Irish, Scottish, English, Cherokee and Osage Indian).

> PEOPLE

10 PEOPLE WHO CONTRACTED SYPHILIS

1. GUSTAVE FLAUBERT.
2. JOHANN WOLFGANG VON GOETHE.
3. HENRY VIII.
4. GUY DE MAUPASSANT.
5. NAPOLEON I.
6. PETER THE GREAT.
7. THE MARQUIS DE SADE.
8. FRANZ SCHUBERT.
9. VINCENT VAN GOGH.
10. OSCAR WILDE.

PEOPLE

10 FAMOUS INSOMNIACS

1. THE EMPEROR CALIGULA.
2. JOSEPH CONRAD.
3. MARLENE DIETRICH.
4. ALEXANDRE DUMAS.
5. W.C. FIELDS.
6. SCOTT FITZGERALD.
7. GALILEO.
8. HERMANN GOERING.
9. RUDYARD KIPLING.
10. ALEXANDER POPE.

Alexandre Dumas suffered terribly from insomnia and tried all sorts of remedies. His most inventive attempt at a cure was to eat an apple under the Arc de Triomphe. It didn't work. Perhaps he should have tried the Eiffel Tower. W.C. Fields used to wrap himself in towels and lie back in a barber's chair because he had always found a trip to the barber's relaxing. On other occasions, he would go out into the garden in the dead of night and turn on the hose so that the spray of the water gently soaked him. Apparently he had always found rain therapeutic.

PEOPLE

20 CHOICE POLITICAL INSULTS

1. 'A triumph of the embalmer's art' (GORE VIDAL on RONALD REAGAN).

2. 'He makes George Bush seem like a personality' (JACKIE MASON on JOHN MAJOR).

3. NANCY ASTOR: 'Winston, if I were your wife, I would put poison in your coffee.'
WINSTON CHURCHILL: 'Nancy, if I were your husband, I would drink it.'

4. 'He is a sheep in sheep's clothing' (WINSTON CHURCHILL on CLEMENT ATTLEE).

5. 'A modest little man with much to be modest about' (CHURCHILL again on ATTLEE).

6. 'He has a bungalow mind' (Former U.S. President THOMAS WOODROW WILSON on his successor WARREN HARDING).

7. 'I feel certain that he would not recognize a generous impulse if he met it on the street' (WILLIAM HOWARD TAFT on his 1912 U.S. Presidential opponent THOMAS WOODROW WILSON).

8. 'He could not see a belt without hitting below it' (MARGOT ASQUITH on DAVID LLOYD GEORGE).

9. 'RICHARD NIXON impeached himself. He gave us Gerald Ford as his revenge' (U.S. politician BELLA ABZUG on Tricky Dickie).

10. 'Nixon's motto was, "If two wrongs don't make a right, try three"' (U.S. writer NORMAN COUSINS).

PEOPLE

11. 'A semi-house-trained polecat' (MICHAEL FOOT on NORMAN TEBBIT).

12. 'A kind of walking obituary for the Labour Party' (CHRIS PATTEN on MICHAEL FOOT).

13. 'If a traveller were informed that such a man was the Leader of the House of Commons, he might begin to comprehend how the Egyptians worshipped an insect' (BENJAMIN DISRAELI on British Prime Minister LORD JOHN RUSSELL).

14. 'GERRY FORD is so dumb that he can't fart and chew gum at the same time' (former U.S. President LYNDON B. JOHNSON).

15. 'He is not only a bore, but he bores for England' (MALCOLM MUGGERIDGE on ANTHONY EDEN).

16. 'I wouldn't say she is open-minded on the Middle East, so much as empty-headed. She probably thinks Sinai is the plural of sinus' (JONATHAN AITKEN on MARGARET THATCHER).

17. 'The self-appointed king of the gutter' (MICHAEL HESELTINE on NEIL KINNOCK).

18. WILLIAM EWART GLADSTONE: 'Mr. Disraeli, you will probably die by the hangman's noose or a vile disease.' BENJAMIN DISRAELI: 'Sir, that depends on whether I embrace your principles or your mistress.'

19. 'HARRY TRUMAN proves that old adage that any man can become President of the United States' (U.S. politician NORMAN THOMAS).

20. 'A shiver looking for a spine to run up' (HAROLD WILSON on EDWARD HEATH).

> PEOPLE

10 FAMOUS PEOPLE AND THEIR PHOBIAS

1. **SID CAESAR** – tonsurphobia, a fear of haircuts.
2. **QUEEN CHRISTINA OF SWEDEN** – fleas.
3. **ELIZABETH I** – anthophobia, a fear of roses.
4. **SIGMUND FREUD** – siderodromophobia, a fear of train travel.
5. **KATHARINE HEPBURN** – dirty hair.
6. **HOWARD HUGHES** – mysophobia, a fear of germs.
7. **MADONNA** – brontophobia, a fear of thunder.
8. **MARILYN MONROE** – agoraphobia, a fear of public places.
9. **RICHIE VALENS** – aerophobia. He died in a plane crash.
10. **NATALIE WOOD** – hydrophobia, a fear of water. She died by drowning.

Queen Christina ruled Sweden in the 17th century and was so terrified of fleas that she ordered the construction of a tiny 10cm-long cannon so that she could spend hours firing miniature cannonballs at the fleas which infested the royal bedchamber. Katharine Hepburn's phobia about dirty hair meant that when she was at Twentieth-Century Fox she apparently used to tour the set sniffing people's hair to make sure that it had been washed. Eccentric millionaire Howard Hughes' obsession with health and hygiene was legendary. Nobody else was permitted to touch his food and any visitors had to stand in a chalk square drawn outside the house and be inspected before being allowed near the front door. His own doctor could only examine him from the other side of the room and, as an added insurance, Hughes would touch nothing without first wrapping his hand in a paper tissue. When he stayed in a hotel, the windows were always darkened and taped. He developed food crazes – eating nothing but ice cream for weeks on end – and only visited a barber twice in ten years.

> PEOPLE

20 SELF-CONFESSED ATHEISTS AND AGNOSTICS

1. DOUGLAS ADAMS.
2. WOODY ALLEN.
3. BILLY BRAGG.
4. MARLON BRANDO.
5. MICHAEL CRICHTON.
6. QUENTIN CRISP.
7. AMANDA DONOHOE.
8. BRIAN ENO.
9. JODIE FOSTER.
10. BILL GATES.
11. MIKHAIL GORBACHEV.
12. BILLY JOEL.
13. STANLEY KUBRICK.
14. SIR IAN McKELLEN.
15. RANDY NEWMAN.
16. JACK NICHOLSON.
17. ROMAN POLANSKI.
18. TERRY PRATCHETT.
19. MICHAEL STIPE.
20. GORE VIDAL.

10 SUPERSTITIOUS PEOPLE

1. **WALT DISNEY** used to wash his hands 30 times an hour.

2. **GEORGE II** was a stickler about timekeeping. At one minute to nine every night, he would stand outside his mistress's bedroom, fob-watch in hand. At precisely nine, he would enter, pull down his breeches and have sex — often without taking off his hat.

3. **CHARLES DICKENS** always touched things three times for luck.

4. **ARNOLD SCHOENBERG** was superstitious about the number 13. Fittingly, the composer died on Friday the 13th at 13 minutes to midnight.

5. **HANS CHRISTIAN ANDERSEN** always turned back twice after leaving a room to ensure that all candles were out. When staying in hotels, he always took with him a coil of rope in case of fire.

6. **LOUIS XIV** hated washing and only took three baths in his whole life.

7. **LORD BADEN-POWELL** was obsessed with washing his entire body daily.

8. **EDWARD VII** had been told by a palmist that the numbers 6 and 9 would guide his life. He married in 1863 (when split this makes 9+9) to a bride, Alexandra, whose name had nine letters, as did that of her father, Christian IX. Edward's coronation took place on August 9, and he reigned for nine years before dying at the age of 69.

9. **GEORGE V** kept the hundreds of clocks at Sandringham House, Norfolk, 30 minutes fast so that he would never be late for an appointment.

10. **PETER ILICH TCHAIKOVSKY**, while conducting, used to hold his chin with his left hand and conduct with his right because he was afraid his head would roll off his shoulders.

PEOPLE

SEPARATED AT BIRTH: 20 PAIRS WHO SHARE THE SAME BIRTHDAY

1. STEPHEN STILLS and VICTORIA PRINCIPAL (January 3, 1945).
2. GEORGE FOREMAN and LINDA LOVELACE (January 10, 1949).
3. PRINCESS MARGARET and JANIS JOPLIN (January 19, 1943).
4. FEDERICO FELLINI and DEFOREST KELLEY (January 20, 1920).
5. NEIL DIAMOND and RAY STEVENS (January 24, 1941).
6. EARTHA KITT and ROGER VADIM (January 26, 1928).
7. ERIC IDLE and JOHN MAJOR (March 29, 1943).
8. MARLON BRANDO and DORIS DAY (April 3, 1924).
9. GENE WILDER and JACKIE STEWART (June 11, 1939).
10. LINDSAY WAGNER and MERYL STREEP (June 22 ,1949).
11. SYLVESTER STALLONE and BURT WARD July 6,1946).
12. JAMES CAGNEY and ERLE STANLEY GARDNER (July 17, 1899).
13. DANNY GLOVER and DON HENLEY (July 22 ,1947).
14. CHRISSIE HYNDE and JULIE KAVNER (September 7, 1951).
15. LUCIANO PAVAROTTI and JOAN RIVERS (October 12, 1935).
16. MARGOT KIDDER and GEORGE WENDT (October 17, 1948).
17. MANFRED MANN and GEOFF BOYCOTT (October 21, 1940).
18. KATE CAPSHAW and ROSEANNE BARR (November 3, 1953).
19. DAVID HEMMINGS and JULIET MILLS (November 21, 1941).
20. JOHN DENVER and BEN KINGSLEY (December 31,1943).

Yes, it's true. Burt Ward, who played Boy Wonder Robin in the *Batman* TV series, was born on the same day as Sylvester Stallone. Holy coincidence!

> PEOPLE

20 PEOPLE KNOWN BY THEIR MIDDLE NAME

1. DANIEL LOUIS ARMSTRONG.
2. RUZ FIDEL CASTRO.
3. EDWARD MONTGOMERY CLIFT.
4. ALFRED ALISTAIR COOKE.
5. DOROTHY FAYE DUNAWAY.
6. WILLIAM CLARK GABLE.
7. SAMUEL DASHIELL HAMMETT.
8. NORVELL OLIVER HARDY.
9. JAMES PAUL McCARTNEY.
10. TERENCE STEVE McQUEEN.
11. KEITH RUPERT MURDOCH.
12. PATRICK RYAN O'NEAL.
13. ELDRED GREGORY PECK.
14. HELEN BEATRIX POTTER.
15. ROBERT OLIVER REED.
16. ERNESTINE JANE RUSSELL.
17. EDITH NORMA SHEARER.
18. MARIE DIONNE WARWICK.
19. HOWARD ANDY WILLIAMS.
20. MARIE DEBRA WINGER.

10 PEOPLE WHO SUFFERED FROM PILES

1. CASANOVA.
2. CARDINAL RICHELIEU.
3. WILLIAM WORDSWORTH.
4. CHARLES DICKENS.
5. KENNETH WILLIAMS.
6. GEORGE II.
7. HENRI DE TOULOUSE-LAUTREC.
8. NAPOLEON I.
9. ANTON CHEKHOV.
10. FYODOR DOSTOEVSKY.

George II's severe constipation proved his downfall. The strain of trying to go to the toilet brought on a fatal heart attack and he died 'on the throne.'

> PEOPLE

10 FAMOUS LAST WORDS

1. **LUDWIG VAN BEETHOVEN, 1827:** 'I shall hear in heaven!' (Beethoven was stone-deaf).

2. **ANDREW BRADFORD,** the publisher of Philadelphia's first newspaper, 1742: 'O Lord, forgive the errata!'

3. **W.C. FIELDS,** who had been flicking through the Bible on his deathbed, 1946: 'I'm looking for a loophole.'

4. **NEVILLE HEATH,** the murderer who requested a glass of whisky as his last wish before being hanged, 1946: 'You might make that a double.'

5. **HENRIK IBSEN,** when his wife suggested that the playwright was looking a little better, 1906: 'On the contrary.'

6. **LIBERACE,** when asked if he wanted to go to church, 1986: 'I wish I could. I'll just stay here and watch my shows.'

7. **KARL MARX,** after his housekeeper had asked whether he had a final message for the world, 1883: 'Go on, get out! Last words are for fools who haven't said enough.'

8. **VISCOUNT PALMERSTON.** The former British Prime Minister's last words in 1865 displayed his sense of irony. 'Die, my dear doctor? That's the last thing I shall do.'

9. **JAMES W. RODGERS,** the Utah murderer when asked if he had any last requests before facing the firing squad, 1960: 'Yes – a bullet-proof vest.'

10. **OSCAR WILDE,** summoning a final champagne, 1900: 'I am dying, as I have lived, beyond my means.'

PEOPLE

10 ROYAL IMPOSTERS

1. ANNA ANDERSON
(Anastasia, daughter of Russian Czar Nicholas II).
2. STELLA CHIAPPINI (Marie Etoile d'Orléans, Queen of France).
3. HORACE COLE (Emperor of Abyssinia).
4. HARRY DOMELA (Grandson of Kaiser Wilhelm).
5. JIM MORAN (Crown Prince of Arabia).
6. KARL WILHELM NAUNDORFF (Louis XVII, heir to French throne).
7. OTREFIEF (Dmitri, younger son of Ivan the Terrible).
8. LAMBERT SIMNEL (Edward, Earl of Warwick).
9. PERKIN WARBECK (Richard, Duke of York).
10. SARAH WILSON
(Princess Susanna Caroline Matilda, sister of
Charlotte, wife of George III).

Caught stealing from Queen Charlotte, Sarah Wilson, a humble royal maid, was exiled to the United States in 1771 where she convinced Americans that she was Charlotte's sister and thus genuine royalty. As such, she was wined and dined wherever she went. Her exploits pale in comparison to those of Horace Cole who, in 1910, set out to play a trick on the Royal Navy. Socialite Cole had a telegram sent to the Navy, warning of the imminent arrival of the Emperor of Abyssinia at Weymouth. In false beards and rented costumes, Cole and his cohorts (among them the future novelist Virginia Woolf) received a formal gun salute and the playing of the Zanzibar national anthem (the Navy didn't know where Abyssinia was) before being piped aboard the Dreadnought. When questioned, they replied 'Bunga-bunga!' to everything. They got away with it despite one joker's moustache slipping and their make-up running in the rain.

PEOPLE

10 MAD ROYALS

1. **GEORGE III** of Great Britain and Ireland was being driven through Windsor Great Park when he ordered his carriage driver to stop. The King got out, walked over to an oak tree, shook hands with one of its branches and talked to it for several minutes. He thought he was talking to the King of Prussia. He ended up in a straitjacket.

2. **PRINCESS ALEXANDRA** of Bavaria was convinced that as a child she had swallowed a full-size grand piano. Nothing could ever shake her from this belief.

3. **LUDWIG II** of Bavaria (1846–86) was Alexandra's nephew. His reign was notable for his decision to reverse night and day. He had a moon painted on his bedroom ceiling and embarked on epic mountain journeys in the dead of night in a golden sleigh, accompanied by coachmen who were forced to dress in the style of Louis XIV. Known as the 'Dream King', he built fairy-tale castles before finally being declared unfit to rule.

4. **OTTO**, younger brother of Ludwig II, decided the only way to preserve his own sanity was to shoot a peasant a day. Every morning he would start taking pot-shots at the peasants working in the royal garden. As staff numbers diminished, one servant was given the task of loading the king's pistol with blanks while another dressed as a peasant and pretended to fall down dead when Otto shot him.

5. **CATHERINE THE GREAT** of Russia (1729–96), discovering that she had dandruff, imprisoned her hairdresser in an iron cage for three years to stop the news spreading. Enchanted by a primrose in the royal garden, she posted a sentry to guard the plant day and night.

PEOPLE

6. **QUEEN JUANA** of Spain worshipped her husband Philip, who died in 1506, so much that she refused to allow him to be buried and had his coffin accompany her wherever she travelled.

7. **FERDINAND II** of Sicily (1810–59) would only allow the country to have its own postage stamps as long as his portrait was not marred by an unsightly franking mark.

8. **PHILIP**, Prince of Calabria, the eldest son of Charles XIII of Spain (1716–88), was mad about gloves and was known to wear 16 pairs at any one time.

9. **CHARLES VI** of France (1368–1422) was convinced he was made of glass. So he hated travelling by coach in case the vibration caused him to shatter into a thousand pieces. He also started prowling the corridors of the royal palace, howling like a wolf, much to the consternation of Queen Isabeau. Deciding that she no longer wished to share the King's bed, Isabeau came up with a humble lookalike, Odette de Champdivers, to take her place. Every night for 30 years, Odette wore the Queen's clothes in the royal bed and Charles never once spotted the deception.

10. **HENRY CHRISTOPHE**, King of Northern Haiti (1767–1820), ordered his guards to prove their loyalty to him by marching over a 200ft-high cliff. Those who obeyed plunged to their deaths; those who refused were tortured and executed. Henry Christophe ended up shooting himself.

PEOPLE

10 GAY MONARCHS (ALLEGEDLY)

1. **WILLIAM II** of England (1087–1100).
2. **RICHARD I** of England (1189–99).
3. **EDWARD II** of England (1307–27).
4. **JOHN II** of France (1350–64).
5. **JAMES III** of Scotland (1469–88).
6. **HENRI III** of France (1574–89).
7. **JAMES I** of England (James VI of Scotland) (1603–25).
8. **LOUIS XIII** of France (1610–43).
9. **MARY II** of England, Scotland and Ireland (1688–94).
10. **ANNE** of Great Britain and Ireland (1702–14).

Louis XIII of France's sexual preferences are thought to have stemmed from an incident at the age of 14 when he was allowed an attempt at carnal relations with his bride-to-be, Anne of Austria. It was a disaster and filled Louis with such a repugnance for physical love that it was another three years before the marriage was finally consummated. While Louis lavished his devotion on his friend the Marquis de Cinq-Mars, his visits to Anne's bed were isolated incidents. So it was almost by chance that they produced a son, the future Louis XIV. Their second son, Philippe, Duke of Orléans, was forced to wear pretty dresses and to play with dolls because Anne had longed for a daughter. Not surprisingly, he too turned out to be somewhat effeminate.

PEOPLE

10 CHILD RULERS

1. **ALFONSO XIII** of Spain (1886–1931) became King at birth. He survived several assassination attempts before fleeing the country in 1931 at the threat of civil war. When General Franco took charge in 1936, Alfonso was reinstated as a 'private citizen', but never returned to Spain alive and died in Rome in 1941.

2. **JOHN I** of France (1316) also became King at birth, but died five days later.

3. **MARY, QUEEN OF SCOTS** (1542–67) became Queen at the age of one week. She also experienced widowhood early, losing her husband when she was just 18.

4. **HENRY VI** of England (1422–61) became King at eight months old.

5. **PETRONILLA** of Aragon (1137–63) was less than a year old when she came to the throne.

6. **ALFONSO XI** of Leon and Castile (1312–50) was King at a year. He died from the Black Death.

7. **JAMES V** of Scotland (1513–42) became King aged one.

8. **SIGURD II** and his half-brother **INGE I** of Norway became joint rulers in 1136 at the ages of two and one respectively.

9. **ISABELLE**, daughter of Charles VI of France, was only seven when she married England's 29-year-old King Richard II in 1396. Three years later, she was a widow.

10. **SHIH HUANG TI** came to power in China as a 13-year-old boy in 222 BC. He built a network of 270 palaces, linked by tunnels, and was so afraid of assassination that he slept in a different palace each night.

PEOPLE

10 CURIOUS ROYAL DEATHS

1. EDWARD II of England (1307–27) met a painful end in Berkeley Castle, Gloucestershire, when three assassins, hired on the orders of his Queen, Isabella, and her lover Roger Mortimer, rammed a long, open-topped deer's horn up the King's backside. With this firmly in position, the red-hot tip of a long-handled poker was inserted through the horn and deep into Edward's bowels. The poker was then withdrawn, reheated and reinserted at least once more. Edward's screams resounded through the castle but, with no marks on his body, death was ascribed to natural causes.

2. ALEXANDROS I of Greece (1917–20) died from blood poisoning after being bitten by his pet monkey.

3. HENRY I of England (1100–35) died after eating a surfeit of lampreys (small eel-like creatures) at a banquet in France.

4. CHARLES VIII of France (1483–98) was noted for his manners. On entering a tennis court at the Chateau d'Amboise, he bowed to his wife and allowed her to proceed first, but, as he raised his head from his magnanimous gesture, he crashed it against a low wooden beam, fracturing his skull and killing him.

5. MITHRIDATES VI of Pontus in Asia Minor (132 BC–63 BC) took small doses of poison throughout his life to develop a resistance should anyone try to poison him. He built up such a strong immunity that when he tried to take his own life to escape the approaching Romans, the poison he took had no effect. Instead he ordered a slave to kill him with a sword.

PEOPLE

6. **HAAKON VII** of Norway (1905–57) slipped on the soap in his marble bath and struck his head fatally on one of the taps.

7. **QUEEN ELEANOR**, dutiful wife of Edward I of England (1272–1307), was so distressed to see her husband lying gravely ill after poison had set into a battle wound that she personally sucked all the poison from the wound. Her brave deed saved the King's life but killed her. Edward was so moved by her sacrifice that he ordered large crosses – subsequently known as 'Eleanor crosses' – to be erected at each of the 12 places where her coffin stopped during its coach journey from Nottinghamshire to London.

8. **KING JOHN** of England (1199–1216) died in an East Anglian abbey after a sumptuous banquet, laid on for him by grateful subjects. The townsfolk of Lynn had just been awarded a handsome contract to supply the royal garrisons and, to repay the King, they rounded off the banquet with his favourite dessert, peaches in cider. Alas, he consumed such a great amount that he suffered violent stomach pains and died a few days later.

9. **MARGARET**, 'Maid of Norway', was nominally declared Queen of Scotland in 1286 but it was not until 1290 that the seven-year-old Queen sailed from Norway to claim her new kingdom. Alas, on the journey across the North Sea, she suffered terrible sea-sickness and died in the Orkneys before ever setting foot on the Scottish mainland.

10. **EDMUND IRONSIDE**, King of Southern England, for just eight months, was murdered in 1016 while sitting on the toilet. He sat on the long wooden lavatory box in his house to empty his bowels, little knowing that an enemy knight, Edric Streona, was lurking in the pit below. As poor Edmund sat down, Streona twice thrust a sword into him.

20 RARELY INVOKED PATRON SAINTS

1. APOLLONIA – toothache.
2. FIACRE – venereal disease and taxi drivers.
3. ANTHONY CLARET – savings banks.
4. GABRIEL – postal services.
5. SEBASTIAN – neighbourhood watch.
6. GENGULF – unhappy marriages.
7. JOHN THE BAPTIST – motorways.
8. LOUISE DE MARILLAC – social workers.
9. JEROME – librarians.
10. VERONICA – laundry workers.
11. MARTIN DE PORRES – hairdressers.
12. JOSEPH OF ARIMATHEA – grave-diggers and funeral directors.
13. CLARE – embroiderers.
14. VITUS – comedians and mental illness.
15. LUKE – butchers.
16. BERNARD OF CLAIRVAUX – beekeepers.
17. ADRIAN NICOMEDIA – arms dealers.
18. BONA – air hostesses.
19. MATTHEW – accountants.
20. BERNARDINO OF SIENA – advertising executives and hoarseness.

> PEOPLE

10 SHORT LIVED MARRIAGES

1. Actress **EVA BARTOK**'s third marriage (her first had been at 15) was to film publicist William Wordsworth, a descendant of the poet. She left him immediately after the wedding ceremony.

2. **ATTILA THE HUN** died on the night after his wedding in 453. It is rumoured that his desire to consummate the marriage proved fatal.

3. Former child star **PATTY DUKE** stayed married to Michael Tell for just 13 days.

4. In January 1994, a Barnsley couple split up 12 hours after the ceremony following a wedding-night row over the bride's ex-boyfriend.

5. Minor actress Jean Acker left **RUDOLPH VALENTINO** on their wedding night.

6. Silent movie star **DAGMAR GODOWSKY** decided to split from her second husband when, immediately after the ceremony, he put his arm around her and asked possessively: 'Who do you belong to now?' She got him to buy her dinner and then she left him.

7. Actress **GREER GARSON** was married to Edward Snelson for a mere five weeks.

8. One of the shortest royal marriages was that between **HENRY VIII** and **ANNE OF CLEVES**. Henry thought she was ugly and had the marriage declared void after six months. He also ordered Thomas Cromwell, who had recommended Anne as a suitable bride, to be beheaded.

9. U.S. actress **JEAN ARTHUR** split from husband Julian Anker after one day.

10. An hour after getting married at Kensington in November 1975, **KATHRYN SLUCKIN** stunned new husband Jerzy and his relatives by announcing at the reception: 'It won't work.' She went to live in a Finchley commune.

> PEOPLE

10 ODD COUPLES

1. 6ft 2in-tall Fabien Pretou towered over his 3ft 1in bride Natalie Lucius at their wedding at Seysinnet-Pariset, France, in April 1990.

2. Harry Stevens, aged 103, married his cousin, 84-year-old Thelma Lucas, at a Wisconsin retirement home in 1984.

3. 6ft 7in Nigel Wilks married 3ft 11in Beverly Russell at Hull in 1984.

4. In 1871, Captain Martin van Buren Bates married Anna Hanen Swan in London. She was 7ft 5½in. tall and he was 7ft 2½in.

5. When Ruth and Kevin Kimber married in 1990, she was 93 and he was 28.

6. Wrestler Giant Haystacks weighed as much as 50 stone in his prime. By contrast, his bride Rita weighed a mere 7st 7lb at their wedding.

7. Minnie Munro, aged 102, married 83-year-old Dudley Reid in New South Wales in 1991.

8. In 1863, American dwarf Charles S. Stratton, better known as General Tom Thumb, married Lavinia Warren. He was 2ft 10in tall and she was 2ft 8in. In 1884, the widowed Lavinia then married Count Primo Magri who was two inches shorter than her first husband at 2ft 8in.

9. In 1994, 26-year-old American supermodel Anna Nicole Smith married 89-year-old millionaire J. Howard Marshall. She was attracted by his kindness.

10. In 1995, following a courtship lasting several months, 100-year-old Samuel Bukoro took the plunge and married 12-year-old Nyamihanda in Uganda.

But these sights at the altar appeared positively normal compared to that at St. Philip's Church, Birmingham, in 1797 where the bride stood naked throughout the ceremony. The reason behind her forsaking a dress and all other clothing was a superstition which held that if a wealthy woman married a man with debts, the creditors would be unable to reclaim their money from her if she was married naked.

PEOPLE

10 MURDEROUS DOCTORS

1. **MORRIS BOLBER** of Philadelphia masterminded the murder of some 30 Italian patients during the 1930s so that he could claim on the insurance. He used a sandbag to induce cerebral haemorrhage in his victims and make death look like natural causes.

2. **PIERRE BOUGRAT** was convicted of murdering Jacques Rumebe, one of his patients, at Marseilles in 1925. Heavily in debt, Bougrat gave him an overdose of mercuric chloride, beat him up and robbed him of 20,000 francs.

3. **ROBERT BUCHANAN** set up in practice in New York in 1886 where he murdered his second wife, brothel-proprietress Anna Sutherland, for a $50,000 inheritance by giving her morphine. He was electrocuted at Sing Sing in 1895.

4. **THOMAS NEILL CREAM**, the Lambeth Poisoner, murdered four prostitutes with strychnine. On the scaffold, he is alleged to have said, 'I am Jack the – ' just as the bolt was drawn.

5. **WILLIAM HENRY KING** of Brighton, Ontario, poisoned his wife with arsenic so that he could have affairs with his patients. He was hanged in 1859.

6. **GEORGE HENRY LAMSON** murdered his brother-in-law by feeding him a slice of Dundee cake spiced with aconite. He was executed at Wandsworth in 1882.

7. **WILLIAM PALMER**, the Staffordshire Poisoner, may have murdered as many as 14 people, mainly with antimony.

8. **EDWARD PRITCHARD** poisoned his wife and mother-in-law with antimony and was hanged in Glasgow in 1865 before a 100,000 crowd, the last public hanging in Scotland.

9. **WALTER WILKINS** bludgeoned his wife to death at their home in Long Beach, Long Island, in 1919. He blamed burglars but was found guilty of murder. He subsequently hanged himself in jail.

10. **ALICE WYNEKOOP**, a 62-year-old Chicago widow, was found guilty of shooting her daughter-in-law, Rheta, in 1933. She was sentenced to 25 years.

10 PEOPLE WHO MISSED THE TITANIC

1. JOHN PIERPONT MORGAN
(owner of the *Titanic*: blamed his absence on ill-health).

2. ROBERT BACON
(U.S. Ambassador to Paris: cited business priorities).

3. FRANK ADELMAN
(his wife had a premonition of danger so they caught a later ship).

4. MR. SHEPHERD
(his wife sent a cable begging him to take another ship).

5. HENRY C. FRICK
(his wife sprained her ankle).

6. J. HORACE HARDING
(preferred the faster *Mauretania*).

7. GEORGE W. VANDERBILT
(his mother-in-law was worried about maiden voyages).

8. JAMES V. O'BRIEN
(detained by a court case in Ireland).

9. BERTRAM SLADE
(crew member: missed the ship after being held up at a Southampton level crossing by a passing goods train).

10. EDWARD W. BILL
(his wife had a premonition of impending doom).

PEOPLE

THE FIRST 10 WOMEN IN SPACE

1. **VALENTINA TERESHKOVA (USSR)** 1963, Vostok VI.

2. **SVETLANA SAVITSKAYA (USSR)** 1982, Soyuz T7.

3. **SALLY RIDE (USA)** 1983, STS-7 Challenger Shuttle.

4. **JUDITH RESNIK (USA)**
September 1984, STS-41-D Discovery Shuttle.

5. **KATHRYN SULLIVAN (USA)**
October 1984, STS-41-G Challenger Shuttle.

6. **ANNA FISHER (USA)** November 1984, STS-51-A Discovery Shuttle.

7. **MARGARET SEDDON (USA)** April 1985, STS-51-D Discovery Shuttle.

8. **SHANNON LUCID (USA)** June 1985, STS-51-G Discovery Shuttle.

9. **LOREN ACTON (USA)** August 1985, STS-51-F Challenger Shuttle.

10. **BONNIE DUNBAR (USA)**
November 1985, STS-61-A Challenger Shuttle.

> PEOPLE

10 ACCURATE PREMONITIONS

1. David Booth, a Cincinnati office manager, phoned American Airlines after having nightmares on ten successive nights about a DC-10 crash. Three days later, on May 25, 1979, an American DC-10 crashed at Chicago, killing 273 people.

2. The night before his attempt to break the world water speed record in *Bluebird* on January 4, 1967, Donald Campbell told a journalist: 'I have the most awful premonition that I'm going to get the chop. I've had the feeling for days.' The following morning, Campbell was killed in a 300 mph crash aboard *Bluebird*.

3. King Wilhelm I of Württemberg completed the building of Rosenstein Castle in 1829 but didn't move in for another 35 years because a gypsy had prophesied that the King would die there. He finally took up residence in the castle in 1864 and died five days later.

4. In 1896, German psychic Madame de Ferriëm had a vision of an impending disaster. She saw bodies being carried out of a coal mine at Dux in Bohemia in bitterly cold weather. Her vision was published in a German newspaper in 1899. The following year, in an extremely cold spell, hundreds of people were killed by an explosion in a coal mine at Dux.

5. In 1980, American actor David Janssen, former star of *The Fugitive*, had a dream in which he saw himself being carried out in a coffin after a heart attack. He consulted a psychic who advised him to go for a check-up, but it was too late. Two days later, Janssen died from a massive heart attack.

6. As Napoleon's troops advanced into Russia in 1812 Countess Toutschkoff, the wife of a Russian general, dreamt that she was in a room at an inn in a strange town. In her dream, her father entered the room, holding her small son by the hand and told her that her husband had been killed by the French. 'He has fallen,' said the father. 'He has

PEOPLE

fallen at Borodino.' After having the same dream twice more, she told her husband and they consulted a map but could find nowhere called Borodino. On September 7, 1812 the Russians engaged the French in a fierce battle at a village called Borodino, west of Moscow. The Countess and her family stayed at a nearby inn while her husband commanded the reserve forces. The following morning, her father came into the room, holding her small son by the hand, and told her that her husband had been slain. 'He has fallen,' he said. 'He has fallen at Borodino.'

7. In May 1812, a Cornish innkeeper had a dream on three successive nights about the shooting of a prominent politician in the House of Commons. He had no idea of the identity of the man in his dream but a friend said the description matched that of the Prime Minister, Spencer Perceval. Several days later, news reached Cornwall that Perceval had been shot dead in the lobby of the House of Commons.

8. Nashville psychic Spencer Thornton correctly predicted the first three horses home in the 1959 Kentucky Derby. Four days before the race, he wrote the names on a piece of paper which was then sealed, unread, in an envelope and placed in a bank vault. The vault was opened after the race and the paper bore the names of the first three finishers.

9. Julia Grant, wife of US General Ulysses S. Grant, woke on the morning of April 14, 1865 with a strong feeling that she and her husband should get out of Washington. General Grant had been due to attend the theatre with President Lincoln that night but his wife was so insistent that he pulled out. Leaving the city, the Grants passed John Wilkes Booth on his way to assassinate Lincoln at the theatre. Grant was also found to be on Booth's death list.

10. Half-way through a financial meeting, just before 5pm on October 7, 1571, Pope Pius V suddenly announced that there had been a Christian victory. Two weeks later on October 21, a messenger from Venice rode into Rome with news that a Christian fleet had vanquished the Turks at Lepanto. The official report of the battle stated that victory had been confirmed shortly before 5pm on October 7.

> PEOPLE

10 MILITARY MISHAPS

1. The Prussian commanders of the 18th century seemed to suffer from poor eyesight. In 1757, a Prussian army was forced to abandon a safe escape route when they saw the road blocked by what they took to be batteries of Austrian artillery. It turned out to be nothing more deadly than a herd of cattle. In the same year, the Prussians failed to press home their advantage against the French when they mistook young fir trees for French infantry marching to the rescue.

2. In 1836, Mexican troops were engaged in skirmishes with the Texans. On the hot afternoon of April 20 of that year, Mexican General Antonio Lopez de Santa Anna ordered his troops to take a siesta, during which the entire Mexican army was routed by the Texans in just 18 minutes.

3. At the Battle of Karansebes in 1788, 10,000 Austrian soldiers were killed or injured by their own side when drunken comrades started shouting that the Turks were upon them. In the darkness and confusion, the Austrians began firing indiscriminately at each other.

4. When the pretender Sultan of Zanzibar, Said Khalid, refused to vacate the palace in 1896, the British fleet declared war. Thirty-eight minutes later, the war was over. Zanzibar's only warship, the ageing *Glasgow*, was sunk by just two shells and the palace was destroyed.

5. In 1916, the much-prized Fort Douaumont at Verdun in France was captured by a single German soldier after the French General Chrétien (pronounced 'cretin') forgot to pass on a message. His orders were to defend the fort to the last man, but when he went on leave he forgot to tell his successor and so the mighty fortress was manned by just a handful of gunners who were taken completely by surprise. Twenty were arrested while attending a lecture!

6. When relations with Bolivia soured in 1865, Queen Victoria ordered the Royal Navy to send six gunboats to Bolivia and sink its fleet. Her admirals quietly pointed out that Bolivia had no coast and therefore no fleet, whereupon the Queen sent for a map and a pair of scissors and cut Bolivia from the world.

PEOPLE

7. When Viking leader Harald Hardrada invaded England in 1066, he quickly defeated the northern militia near York and waited for the big showdown with King Harold II who was on the south coast anticipating a Norman invasion. Not expecting the English troops for days, Hardrada and his men camped on meadows either side of the River Derwent at Stamford Bridge and, since it was such a lovely day, many of the Vikings removed their armour and indulged in a spot of sunbathing. They didn't even rouse themselves when they saw approaching soldiers, presuming them to be a detachment of Vikings. By the time they realized it was the English army, it was too late. The Vikings were overwhelmed and Hardrada was killed.

8. During the Second World War, the Russians invented the 'dog mine.' The idea was to train dogs to associate food with the underneath of tanks and thus, with bombs strapped to their backs, to wreak havoc on the German Panzer divisions. Alas, the dogs associated food solely with Russian tanks and forced an entire Soviet division to retreat. The plan was quickly scrapped.

9. Famous American General Thomas 'Stonewall' Jackson was devoutly religious and considered fighting on a Sunday to be sinful. In 1862, at the height of the Battle of Mechanicsville in the American Civil War, he stood alone praying on a nearby hill, steadfastly refusing to speak to anyone all afternoon. With nobody to guide them, his Confederate troops suffered huge losses.

10. Japanese soldier Hiroo Onoda continued fighting the Second World War until 1974 from the remote Philippine island of Lubang. Resisting all attempts to make him surrender, he dismissed stories that the war was over as cunning American propaganda. Search parties were greeted with a hail of bullets and it was only when his old commanding officer, Major Yoshimi Taniguchi, flew out to Lubang and ordered him to lay down his arms that Onoda finally complied.

CREATURES

ALL CREATURES GREAT AND SMALL

10 SPIDERS TO AVOID

1. BRAZILIAN HUNTSMAN.
2. SYDNEY FUNNELWEB (Australia).
3. RED-BACK SPIDER (Australia).
4. BLACK WIDOW (Europe and the Americas).
5. TARANTULA (Europe and the Americas).
6. BROWN RECLUSE SPIDER (Americas).
7. WHITE-TAILED SPIDER (Australia).
8. SPITTING SPIDER (The tropics).
9. WOODLOUSE SPIDER (Europe).
10. *SICARIUS HAHNII* (South Africa).

Although nearly all spiders are venomous, only a handful are dangerous to humans. The American black widow is 15 times more venomous than a rattlesnake but the strongest venom is thought to be that of the Brazilian huntsman, a particularly aggressive species. It likes to hide in shoes and clothes, and a huntsman is said to have killed two Brazilian children when it got into their bed one night. The legendary tarantula (a large wolf spider) gets its name from its links with the Italian town of Taranto. Its bite was believed to be fatal unless victims danced furiously until they dropped from sheer exhaustion. Tarantella dancing is still popular in Italy, although the tarantula has been much-maligned since its bite causes nothing more than a sharp pain. The deadly spider from legend was more than likely a different species altogether – the European black widow.

> CREATURES

THE 10 MOST VENOMOUS SNAKES IN THE WORLD

1. THE FIERCE SNAKE (Australia).
2. ISLAND FER-DE-LANCE (Brazil).
3. BLACK MAMBA (Southern and Central Africa).
4. TAIPAN (Australia and New Guinea).
5. TIGER SNAKE (Australia).
6. COMMON KRAIT (Southern Asia).
7. DEATH ADDER (Australia).
8. BROWN SNAKE (Australia).
9. CARPET VIPER (Africa and Asia).
10. BEAKED SEA SNAKE (Pacific Ocean).

A single male fierce snake possesses enough venom to kill 250,000 mice. Fortunately it lives in the remotest part of the Australian outback where it hardly ever comes into contact with man. As a result, there have never been any human fatalities although a bite would undoubtedly be lethal if only because medical aid would take so long to arrive. The island fer-de-lance, which inhabits a small island off the coast of Brazil, feeds entirely on sparrows and must possess a strong venom so that a bitten bird falls near enough for the snake to eat it. The mainland fer-de-lance, whilst still a formidable adversary, has slightly less potent venom. Of the snakes which come into contact with man, the black mamba is probably the most feared on account of its size and speed. Yet the snake which is probably responsible for more human deaths than any other is the saw-scaled or carpet viper because it is relatively common and lives around highly-populated regions.

CREATURES

10 SNAKES WHICH EAT OTHER SNAKES

1. NORTH AMERICAN KINGSNAKE.
2. TEXAS CORAL SNAKE.
3. RING-NECKED SNAKE.
4. SHARP-TAILED SNAKE.
5. KING COBRA.
6. KRAIT.
7. ASIAN CORAL SNAKE.
8. BLACK-HEADED PYTHON.
9. PAPUAN PYTHON.
10. BURROWING ASP.

If the need arises, quite a few breeds of snake will eat other species – it is not unknown for a grass snake to devour an adder – but the above ten specialize in a diet of serpents. The North American kingsnake is particularly bold and will even attack a deadly rattlesnake since it has a degree of immunity from the rattlesnake's venom. The sharp-tailed snake feeds mainly on the crowned snake of Florida while the burrowing asp has specialized fangs which enable it to bite its prey in confined spaces. Thus it is particularly fond of other burrowing snakes, especially the slim-collared snake. Pythons are renowned for being able to devour huge animals – a pig is a mere snack to a fully-grown python – and a Papuan python was once found with a carpet python in its stomach.

CREATURES

20 CREATURES WHICH MATE FOR LIFE

1. GIBBON.
2. GORILLA.
3. ORANG-UTAN.
4. BEAVER.
5. HOODED SEAL.
6. BADGER.
7. FOX.
8. MONGOOSE.
9. TERMITE.
10. SWAN.
11. STORK.
12. ALBATROSS.
13. PENGUIN.
14. JACKDAW.
15. GREY GOOSE.
16. MONTAGUE'S HARRIER.
17. BUDGERIGAR.
18. LOVEBIRD.
19. VULTURE.
20. PIGEON.

CREATURES

10 CREATURES WITH THEIR OWN LIGHTS

1. FIREFLY.
2. GLOW-WORM.
3. SEA ANEMONE.
4. CORAL SHRIMP.
5. SQUID.
6. INDO-PACIFIC FISH.
7. BATHYSPHERE FISH.
8. HATCHET FISH.
9. LANTERN FISH.
10. ANGLER FISH.

The angler fish lives in the depths of the Atlantic where there is no light. Above its mouth is a bony projection and from this stretches a long, thin line like a fishing rod, the end of which is illuminated by bacteria. The angler fish waves this rod about, causing smaller fish to investigate in the belief that the moving light is food. All the while, the angler fish keeps its body perfectly still...until the tiny fish come within eating distance. The hatchet fish emits greenish-white lights which, because they look like a row of teeth, deter predators, and the bathysphere fish is so-called because the pale blue, glowing spots along its sides resemble the portholes of a diving-bell. It has two long tentacles with luminous ends which attract the fish on which it feeds. Fireflies glow in the dark to attract mates but, placed inside perforated gourd lanterns, have been used as a form of cheap lighting in places like Brazil and China. The glow from six large fireflies provides enough light to read a book.

CREATURES

10 MASTERS OF CAMOUFLAGE

1. CHAMELEON.
2. STICK INSECT.
3. PRAYING MANTIS.
4. ELEPHANT HAWK MOTH.
5. LEAF INSECT.
6. COPPERBAND BUTTERFLY FISH.
7. KING PAGE BUTTERFLY.
8. CRANE-FLY.
9. HORNED TOAD.
10. ROCK PTARMIGAN.

When threatened, the caterpillar of the elephant hawk moth retracts its legs and rolls over to reveal a pair of false 'eyes' like a deadly pit viper. Wisely, the predator tends to keep its distance. The caterpillar of the king page butterfly has an equally effective although less intimidating disguise – bird droppings. The pupa of the crane-fly, which lives in tropical rain forests, camouflages itself as a drop of water and hangs from the edge of a palm leaf, while the leaf insect has markings which resemble the veins of a leaf. For added authenticity, it has blotches to look like the holes in a leaf and its body has a brown edging to suggest a dying leaf. Like the chameleon, the horned toad changes colour to blend in with its surroundings – in this case, desert rocks. The copperband butterfly fish is designed in such a way that an enemy will think its tail is its head and will therefore snap at the wrong end. The fish also has a false eye near the tail, its real eye being concealed in a dark vertical stripe.

CREATURES

THE 10 FASTEST BIRDS IN THE WORLD

1. SPINE-TAILED SWIFT: 106mph.

2. FRIGATE BIRD: 95mph.

3. SPUR-WINGED GOOSE: 88mph.

4. RED-BREASTED MERGANSER: 80mph.

5. WHITE-RUMPED SWIFT: 77mph.

6. CANVASBACK DUCK: 72mph.

7. EIDER DUCK: 70mph.

8. TEAL: 68mph.

9= MALLARD: 65mph.

PINTAIL: 65mph.

CREATURES

10 SEX MACHINES

1. DESERT RAT.
2. MULTIMAMMATE RAT.
3. COD.
4. MUSSEL.
5. LEMMING.
6. RABBIT.
7. PRAIRIE DOG.
8. MOLE RAT.
9. FRUIT FLY.
10. TERMITE.

The desert rat is the ultimate sex machine, a creature which makes the rabbit look positively celibate. For the desert rat has sex as often as 122 times per hour. Blessed with no fewer than 24 teats, the multimammate rat can give birth to up to 120 offspring per year. Even this is small fry compared to certain insects and sea creatures. A termite is capable of laying an egg every two seconds while a mussel can produce 25 million eggs at a time and a cod eight million at a time. You'd need a lot of chips to go with that! A pair of Indian pythons were once observed copulating for 180 days and stick insects aren't usually in much of a hurry either. They have been known to keep it up for 79 successive days. The poor old Scandinavian lemmings become so agitated by the number of young in the colony that a fear of overcrowding is thought to be the reason behind their mass march of self-destruction. Desperate to reach the wide-open spaces of the sea, many plunge headlong to their deaths over cliffs while others drown *en route* trying to cross rivers.

> CREATURES

10 CREATURES WITH ODD SEXUAL HABITS

1. After mating, the male garter snake from North America seals up the female's sexual opening with a plug made from kidney secretions. This acts as a form of chastity belt, ensuring that the female is fertilized by the first male to mate with her.

2. The male Darwin's frog, found on the southern coast of Chile, swallows the eggs his mate lays and keeps them in a sac under his chin. When the tadpoles are big enough, he opens his mouth and releases them.

3. The seahorse is the only creature where the male becomes pregnant. When ready to breed, the female inserts a nipple-like appendage into the male and releases her eggs into a special pouch in his stomach. He then discharges his sperm over them and, once the eggs are fertilized, his belly takes on the rounded shape.

4. For the mouthbrooder catfish, which lives off Mozambique, fertilisation takes place in the female's mouth. She releases her ova into the water and then turns round and swallows them. When the male swims by, she mistakes the distinctive spots on his anal fin for more eggs. As she opens her mouth to swallow them, she ends up catching his sperm instead. The young fish remain in the mouth until they have absorbed their egg yolk before finally venturing out to feed. Even then, they often return to the safety of the mouth at night or if they feel threatened.

5. Since the female bedbug has no sexual opening, the male drills his own vagina, using his curved, pointed penis as a drill. The male then inserts his sperm and the blood-sucking female feeds on some of it when blood is in short supply.

CREATURES

6. The female praying mantis eats her partner after sex. During copulation, the larger female hooks her deadly arms around him and begins nibbling away at him. Sometimes she doesn't even wait until copulation has finished before turning him into her next meal, but his sex drive is so strong that he can carry on even while being eaten.

7. The male moth mite is born as a mature insect and at birth helps his mother by seizing his sisters as they emerge from the sexual cavity and dragging them out of the birth passage with his hind legs. He then mates with them and continues to hover around his mother's birth passage ready to snap up the next batch of sisters.

8. The legs of the male water mite sometimes double as sexual organs and can be used to penetrate the female. While mating, he pins the female to the ground with tiny hooks so that she can barely move. He also glues himself to her with a special secretion so that there is no escape.

9. The male swamp antechinus, a mouse-like marsupial from Australia, is the only mammal which dies after mating. The males dedicate their lives to a round of non-stop copulation until they literally drop dead. The majority die of starvation because they have no time to feed between sex.

10. The male tick doesn't have a penis so instead he pokes around in the female's vagina with his nose. When her opening is large enough, he turns around and deposits sperm from his rear on to the entrance of her orifice. He then uses his nose to push the sperm deeper into the vagina.

CREATURES

10 COUNTRIES WHERE SHEEP OUTNUMBER PEOPLE

1. FALKLAND ISLANDS.
2. NEW ZEALAND.
3. AUSTRALIA.
4. URUGUAY.
5. MONGOLIA.
6. SYRIA.
7. NAMIBIA.
8. ICELAND.
9. MAURITANIA.
10. SOMALIA.

Whoever has stayed awake long enough to count the world's sheep estimates that there are in the region of 1,200,000,000 which works out at an average of around one sheep for every four people. However, in certain countries the ratio is definitely in favour of the sheep – nowhere more so than the Falkland Islands with a human population of under 2,000 but a sheep population of 700,000, making 350 sheep for every person. In New Zealand, there are approximately 20 sheep per human and in Australia, around ten. Lower down the list, Iceland boasts a ratio of three sheep per person and even Ireland has 1.7 woolly-heads for every human specimen.

CREATURES

20 PLANTS AND THEIR MEANINGS
(AS STATED IN AN 1845 AMERICAN FLORAL VOCABULARY)

1. ANEMONE: frailty.
2. BARBERRY: sourness.
3. BASIL: hatred.
4. BINDWEED: humility.
5. BLUEBELL: constancy.
6. BUTTERCUP: ingratitude.
7. CARNATION: disdain.
8. DAHLIA: dignity.
9. DAISY: innocence.
10. HAREBELL: grief.
11. JONQUIL: desire.
12. LARKSPUR: fickleness.
13: LETTUCE: cold-heartedness.
14. LILY: purity.
15. LUPIN: sorrow.
16. NETTLE: slander.
17: POLYANTHUS: confidence.
18: YELLOW ROSE: infidelity.
19: ST. JOHN'S WORT: animosity.
20. VENUS FLY TRAP: deceit.

The moral is simple. If you want to impress your loved one, never present her with a lettuce as a token of your admiration.

CREATURES

10 PECULIAR PLANTS AND TREES

1. The sausage tree of Africa *(Kigelia africana)* gets its name from the long, thick fruits which hang from the tree like sausages. The fruits have a different connotation to the Ashanti people of Ghana who call it the 'hanging breast tree', comparing it to old tribeswomen whose life of unremitting breastfeeding results in very long breasts.

2. The starfish flower (*Stapelia variegata*) from Africa looks like a brown and yellow starfish nestling in the sand. It also smells like a dead animal, as a result of which flies, thinking it's a lump of rotten meat, decide it is the perfect place to raise a family. As they lay their eggs on the surface, they inadvertently pollinate the flower at the same time.

3. *Welwitschia mirabilis*, from the deserts of Namibia, can live for over 2,000 years, yet its central trunk never grows more than 3ft in height. Instead the energy is transmitted into its two huge leaves which never fall and continue growing throughout the plant's life. The leaves can be as long as 20ft.

4. The banyan tree *(Ficus benghalensis)* of India has more than one trunk. When the tree attains a certain size, it sends down rope-like roots which, on reaching the soil, take root and then thicken to form additional trunks. So the tree can spread outwards almost indefinitely.
A 200-year-old specimen in the Calcutta Botanic Gardens has over 1,700 trunks, whilst during Alexander the Great's Indian campaign 20,000 soldiers are said to have sheltered under a single banyan tree.

5. The merest touch causes the sensitive plant (*Mimosa pudica*) to collapse in one-tenth of a second. The wilting pose deters grazing

CREATURES

animals from eating it and ten minutes later, when the danger has passed, the plant reverts to its upright position.

6. *Puya raimondii* of Bolivia can take up to 150 years to bloom. And once it has flowered, it promptly dies. Although it's a herbaceous plant, it is built like a tree with a stem strong enough to support a man.

7. The grapple tree (*Harpagophytum procumbens*) of South Africa produces a fearsome fruit called the 'Devil's Claw' which has been known to kill a lion. The fruit is covered in fierce hooks which latch on to passing animals. In trying to shake the fruit off, the animal disperses the seeds but at the same time, the hooks sink deeper into the creature's flesh. If the animal touches the fruit with its mouth, the fruit will attach itself to the animal's jaw, inflicting great pain and preventing it from eating. Antelopes are the usual victims.

8. The national flower of South Africa, the sugarbush (*Protea repens*), depends on forest fires for survival. When its seeds have been fertilized, they are encased inside tough fireproof bracts which don't reopen until they have been scorched by fire. When the fire has passed, the seeds emerge undamaged.

9. As it reaches upwards, the trunk of California's boojum tree (*Idris columnaris*) gradually reduces to a series of long, tentacle-like protuberances. Sometimes these droop down to the ground and root so that the tree forms a complete arch. The tree has no branches but is instead covered with thorny stems.

10. When the fruit of the South American sandbox tree (*Hura crepitans*) is ripe, it explodes with such force that the seeds can be scattered up to 15ft from the main trunk. The explosion is so loud that it can scare the life out of unsuspecting passers-by.

> CREATURES

10 CARNIVOROUS PLANTS

1. ALABAMA CANEBRAKE PITCHER PLANT.

2. BLADDERWORT.

3. BUTTERWORT.

4. COBRA LILY.

5. HOODED PITCHER.

6. HUNTSMAN'S HORN.

7. PINK FAN.

8. SUNDEW.

9. SWEET TRUMPET.

10. VENUS FLY TRAP.

The pitcher plant not only eats insects but is also capable of devouring small animals such as the rats and frogs which inhabit the Malaysian forests where it lives. The plant's leaves are shaped to form a pitcher, the inside of which has a slippery, waxy surface which reduces the chance of a creature's escape. The largest pitchers can be as much as 20in high and have special glands which secrete digestive juices. The plant acts as a stomach and can digest all the soft parts of the creature's body as well as absorbing its nutritional substances. It takes no more than a few days for the plant to devour completely a piece of meat thrown into the pitcher. Pitchers are also ideal for storing water and monkeys are often seen drinking from them, hence the plant's alternative name of 'monkey cup'.

CREATURES

10 FREAK PETS

1. THE SPHINX CAT. Bred from a Canadian mutation, it is virtually hairless and has a damaged spine which results in a hopping walk coveted by connoisseurs of the breed.

2. The CROP PIGEON is bred with an over-sized crop and absurdly long feathers on its feet. The crop can't be cleaned naturally and the bird finds walking difficult.

3. POSITION CANARIES are bred to resemble the figures 1 and 7. Parts of their bodies are featherless and their over-stretched tendons mean they shift continually from foot to foot.

4. The MUNCHKIN CAT has short hind legs and three-inch front legs. It can hardly jump, can't groom itself and suffers from premature ageing of its long spine.

5. The CHINESE CRESTED DOG, once bred for the table, is almost hairless. As a result, it suffers from the cold.

6. The SHAR PEI, a dog designed in the US from a Chinese strain, is bred for its wrinkles.

7. A German breed of LOP-EARED RABBIT has ears as long as its body, rendering walking difficult.

8. PERSIAN CATS are bred to have 'piggy' faces. The nose is little more than a stump.

9. MUTANT GOLDFISH are deliberately bred with large growths on their faces.

10. TERRAPINS have been bred with two heads.

CREATURES

10 CELEBRITY STEEDS

1. SILVER (The Lone Ranger).
2. SCOUT (Tonto).
3. TRIGGER (Roy Rogers).
4. BUTTERMILK (Dale Evans).
5. DIABLO (The Cisco Kid).
6. LOCO (Pancho).
7. RAWHIDE (The Range Rider).
8. LUCKY (Dick West).
9. TOPPER (Hopalong Cassidy).
10. MARSHAL (Matt Dillon)

Roy Rogers was so devoted to Trigger that when the horse died he had it stuffed and mounted. Hopalong Cassidy, known affectionately as Hoppy, was played on TV by the ageing William Boyd and had his own code of conduct for youngsters, emphasising the virtues of loyalty, honesty, kindness and ambition. And the Lone Ranger was considered such an epitome of American honesty and decency that Clayton Moore, who played the Masked Man, was later invited to the White House to meet that other pillar of American honesty and decency, Richard Nixon. Moore also made a good living out of opening supermarkets at $4,000 a time – it was extra if they wanted the horse.

CREATURES

10 ANIMALS WHICH HAD THEIR OWN TV SERIES

1. **LASSIE**, the collie bitch.
2. **BLACK BEAUTY**, the horse.
3. **RIN TIN TIN**, the Alsatian.
4. **CHAMPION THE WONDER HORSE.**
5. **FLIPPER**, the dolphin.
6. **SALTY**, the sea lion.
7. **FURY**, the black stallion.
8. **SKIPPY, THE BUSH KANGAROO.**
9. **GENTLE BEN**, the bear.
10. **MY FRIEND FLICKA**, the horse.

Lassie was treated like a Hollywood star. She lived in an air-conditioned kennel and was insured for $100,000. On the set, she rested on a mobile bed between takes. She needed to conserve her energy, for it was calculated that by 1960 she had brought 152 villains to justice, rescued 73 animals and birds, leapt through 47 windows, off 13 cliffs and on to 17 moving vehicles. Similarly, Rin Tin Tin had a valet, a personal chef, a limousine and a chauffeur for his exclusive use. He also had his own five-room dressing-room complex on the studio lot. Flipper, known originally as Susie, beat off 80 other dolphins to win the coveted role. No doubt there was some backstage bitching over the bucket of herrings that night! And one of Skippy's co-stars was a young Liza Goddard. It was an experience she will never forget. 'I was weed on by a wombat and I got lice either from an emu or a koala bear. I had to wash in DDT.'

> CREATURES

10 HEROIC ANIMALS

1. **PRISCILLA THE PIG.** Owned by Victoria Herberta of Houston, Texas (with whom she sometimes shared a bed), Priscilla hit the headlines in 1984 when she rescued an 11-year-old boy from drowning. Paddling in Lake Somerville, Priscilla spotted that young Anthony Melton was in difficulties and swam to his assistance. She used her snout to keep the boy's head above water until he could hold on to her collar and then dragged him to the safety of the shore.

2. **NIPPER THE COLLIE.** When fire broke out at Ansty Farm, Sussex, in 1985, Nipper, the farm's five-year-old collie, saved calves and lambs by repeatedly venturing into the smoke and shepherding them to safety. As a result of the ordeal, the brave dog ended up with singed fur and blistered paws.

3. **CARLETTA THE COW.** At his Tuscany farm in 1986, Bruno Cipriano's pet cow, Carletta, saved him being gored by a boar when she charged at the beast and butted it with her horns.

4. **BRACKEN THE COLLIE.** In 1983 Ian Elliot was chopping down trees on his Canadian farm when a pine tree crashed on to him, breaking his back. His live was saved by his faithful sheepdog Bracken who lay across his stricken master to maintain his body temperature. Then, when Bracken heard the sound of voices in the distance, he ran to the men and led them back to the injured Mr. Elliot.

5. **LEO THE POODLE.** In 1984 Leo, a four-year-old standard poodle, was out playing near his home in Hunt, Texas, with young brother and sister Sean and Erin Callahan when the trio encountered a rattlesnake. As the snake attacked, Leo leapt between it and 11-year-old Sean, enabling the boy to escape. Although receiving six potentially deadly bites to the head, Leo somehow survived.

CREATURES

6. BRUCE THE LABRADOR/ALSATIAN. When a four-year-old Dyfed boy got stuck in riverside mud and sank up to his armpits, Bruce cleverly lay on his side and gripped the boy's shoulder in his mouth to stop him sinking further into the mire. Fortunately, the boy's mother spotted their predicament and organised a rescue.

7. BARRY THE ST. BERNARD. During his 12-year career working in the Swiss Alps, Barry rescued more than 40 people, among them a small boy trapped beneath an avalanche which had killed his mother. Barry spread himself across the boy's frozen body to keep him warm and licked his face until he woke up. To complete the rescue, Barry carried the boy to the nearest house.

8. A SCHOOL OF DOLPHINS. In 1989 Adam Maguire was surfing near Sydney when he was attacked by a shark. As the shark moved in for the kill, it was distracted by a school of dolphins thrashing around in the water. To prevent the shark reaching its prey, the dolphins then swam around it in circles until Adam's friends had managed to rescue him.

9. WOODIE THE COLLIE CROSS. Ray Thomas of Cleveland, Ohio, and his fiancée Rae Anne Knitter were walking along a nature trail in the Rocky River Reservation one day in 1980 when Ray climbed to the top of a cliff to take some photographs. As he disappeared from sight, Rae Anne's collie cross, Woodie, began straining uncharacteristically on the lead. Eventually Woodie broke free and raced up the hill in Ray's footsteps. Rae Anne followed and spotted Ray lying unconscious in a stream at the foot of the 80ft cliff. With him was Woodie who had jumped off the cliff (breaking both hips in the process) and was nudging Ray's head to keep it above water. Both man and dog survived.

10. THE UNNAMED RABBIT. Hearing the family's pet rabbit scratching at its hutch, Tanya Birch woke up to find that her block of flats at Wisbech, Cambridgeshire, was on fire. She grabbed her two-year-old daughter, Heather, and fled to safety. Sadly, the rabbit died in the blaze.

MUSIC, FILM AND TV

20 BANDS AND THEIR ORIGINAL NAMES

1. BLUR (Seymour).
2. RADIOHEAD (On A Friday).
3. STATUS QUO (The Spectres).
4. THE BEACH BOYS (Carl and the Passions).
5. PROCUL HARUM (The Paramounts).
6. DAVE DEE, DOZY, BEAKY, MICK AND TICH (Dave Dee and the Bostons).
7. TALKING HEADS (The Artistics).
8. MARMALADE (Dean Ford and the Gaylords).
9. THE BYRDS (The Beefeaters).
10. THE WHO (The High Numbers).
11. MIDDLE OF THE ROAD (Los Caracas).
12. DEPECHE MODE (Composition of Sound).
13. SLADE (Ambrose Slade).
14. THE BAY CITY ROLLERS (The Saxons).
15. BLONDIE (The Stilettos).
16. CHICAGO (Chicago Transit Authority).
17. BLACK SABBATH (Earth).
18. MADNESS (The Invaders).
19. KAJAGOOGOO (Art Nouveau).
20. JOHNNY KIDD AND THE PIRATES (Freddie Heath and the Nutters).

MUSIC, FILM AND TV

HOW 10 BANDS GOT THEIR NAMES

1. **DURAN DURAN** took their name from the villain in Jane Fonda's 1968 film *Barbarella* since many of the early gigs were played at Barbarella's club in Birmingham.

2. **LYNYRD SKYNYRD** named themselves after Leonard Skinner, an unpopular gym teacher at their school.

3. **LED ZEPPELIN** were known as the New Yardbirds until they heard one of Keith Moon's favourite phrases: 'That went down like a lead Zeppelin'.

4. **FRANKIE GOES TO HOLLYWOOD** chose their name from an old newspaper story about Frank Sinatra moving into films.

5. **T'PAU** were named after Mr. Spock's Vulcan friend in *Star Trek*.

6. **THIN LIZZY** adopted their name from the robot Tin Lizzie who appeared in the *Beano* comic. They added the 'h' because they reckoned it wouldn't be sounded in Ireland.

7. **BREAD** came up with their name after being stuck in traffic behind a Wonder Bread lorry.

8. **PROCUL HARUM** were named after a friend's pedigree cat.

9. **CROWDED HOUSE** took their name from a cramped apartment they once shared.

10. **TALKING HEADS** saw a listing in a TV guide which referred to the 'talking heads' taking part in a TV debate.

According to Jonathan King, owner of their record label, 10CC got their name from the average amount of semen contained in male ejaculation.

10 MUSICIANS WHO WERE MURDERED

1. SONNY BOY WILLIAMSON – U.S. harmonica player murdered in Chicago in 1948.

2. LITTLE WALTER – U.S. blues singer who suffered a fatal head injury following a fight in 1968.

3. JAMES SHEPPARD – the founder of U.S. group Shep and the Limelites, he was found dead in his car on the Long Island Expressway in 1970 after being attacked and robbed.

4. KING CURTIS – U.S. saxophonist stabbed to death in 1971.

5. AL JACKSON – the drummer with Booker T and The MGs was shot by burglars in 1975.

6. SAL MINEO – stabbed to death while walking home in Los Angeles in 1976.

7. JOHN LENNON – shot outside his New York home in 1980 by Mark Chapman, to whom he had given his autograph only a few hours earlier.

8. SAMUEL GEORGE – drummer with U.S. group The Capitols suffered fatal stab wounds in 1982.

9. MARVIN GAYE – shot dead by his father during a bitter row in 1984.

10. PETER TOSH – shot by burglars in 1987.

Sam Cooke was another to meet a violent end. Following a party in 1964, Cooke inadvertently stepped into the wrong motel room while in a state of undress. The manageress, who lived in that room, felt threatened by his presence and shot him dead.

MUSIC, FILM AND TV

10 WAYS IN WHICH THE NUMBER 9 AFFECTED JOHN LENNON'S LIFE

1. He and his son Sean were both born on October 9.

2. His mother lived at 9 Newcastle Road, Wavertree, Liverpool.

3. As a student, he took the number 72 bus from his home to Liverpool Art College (7+2 = 9).

4. Future manager Brian Epstein first attended a Beatles concert at the Cavern in Liverpool on November 9, 1961 and clinched a record contract with EMI on May 9, 1962.

5. The group's first hit, 'Love Me Do', was on Parlophone disc 4949.

6. Lennon met Yoko Ono on November 9, 1966.

7. Their New York apartment was on West 72nd Street and their Dakota 8. home was number 72 (7+2 = 9).

8. His fixation with the number 9 often manifested itself in his songs, 9 of which included titles such as 'Number 9 Dream', 'Revolution 9' and 'One After 909'.

9. He was shot dead by Mark Chapman late on the evening of December 8, 1980 in New York but the five-hour time difference meant that it was December 9 in Liverpool.

10. His body was taken to the Roosevelt Hospital on New York's Ninth Avenue.

MUSIC, FILM AND TV

10 PEOPLE WHO HAVE HAD A SONG WRITTEN ABOUT THEM

1. **DON McLEAN** – Killing Me Softly With His Song, Roberta Flack.
2. **RITA COOLIDGE** – Delta Lady, Joe Cocker.
3. **WARREN BEATTY** – You're So Vain, Carly Simon.
4. **SYD BARRETT** – Shine On You Crazy Diamond, Pink Floyd.
5. **CAROLE KING** – Oh Carol, Neil Sedaka.
6. **ANGIE BOWIE** – Angie, The Rolling Stones.
7. **CHRISTIE BRINKLEY** – Uptown Girl, Billy Joel.
8. **PATTI BOYD** – Layla, Derek and the Dominos.
9. **BRIAN EPSTEIN** – Baby You're A Rich Man, The Beatles.
10. **BUDDY HOLLY** – American Pie, Don McLean.

In addition to 'Baby You're A Rich Man', it is thought that John Lennon also wrote 'You've Got To Hide Your Love Away' for the Beatles' gay manager Brian Epstein after Epstein had made a pass at Lennon on holiday in Spain in spring 1963. Lennon penned the song on their return to England. Intense speculation surrounded the identity of the subject of 'You're So Vain' until Carly Simon finally admitted that 'There is nothing in the lyric which isn't true of Warren Beatty.' Pink Floyd dedicated 'Shine On You Crazy Diamond' to their erstwhile member, the reclusive Syd Barrett – it appeared on their album 'Wish You Were Here'. And after Neil Sedaka had written 'Oh Carol', Carole King replied with her own ditty, 'Oh Neil'...

MUSIC, FILM AND TV

10 MUSICIANS KILLED IN ROAD ACCIDENTS

1. EDDIE COCHRAN, 1960.
2. JOHNNY KIDD, 1966.
3. DUANE ALLMAN, 1971.
4. DICKIE VALENTINE, 1971.
5. CLARENCE WHITE (The Byrds), 1973.
6. MARC BOLAN, 1977.
7. HARRY CHAPIN, 1981.
8. DAVE PRATER (Sam and Dave), 1988.
9. PETE DE FREITAS (Echo and the Bunnymen), 1989.
10. COZY POWELL, 1998.

Eddie Cochran was killed at the age of 21 in a car crash at Chippenham, Wiltshire, on his way to London Airport and a flight back to the U.S. following a tour of England. Ironically, he had just recorded 'Three Steps To Heaven' which promptly became a posthumous Number One for him in the U.K. Duane Allman was killed in a motorbike accident in Macon, Georgia. By a macabre coincidence, fellow-Allman Brothers member Berry Oakley was killed in another motorbike crash just three blocks away a year later. The most famous rock shrine in the U.K. is the tree in Richmond, Surrey, into which the car carrying Marc Bolan crashed on September 16, 1977. Since then, the anniversary of his death has been marked by ribbons being tied to the tree and floral tributes laid at its base.

MUSIC, FILM AND TV

10 ROCK ECCENTRICS

1. **IAN ANDERSON.** The Jethro Tull singer with the wild eyes often used to walk around Luton with a lampshade on his head.

2. **ROKY ERICKSON.** Singer/guitarist with psychedelic Texan band The Thirteenth Floor Elevators. Erickson was convinced that he was an alien from Mars and consulted a lawyer to have this fact acknowledged officially.

3. **KEITH MOON.** Late drummer with The Who. Renowned for his wild behaviour, his speciality was dumping Rolls-Royces in swimming pools.

4. **PRINCE.** The diminutive popster has had more aliases than the Great Train Robbers – from 'Prince' to a squiggle, to 'The artist formerly known as Prince' to simply 'The artist.' Having changed his name to the squiggle, he proceeded to shout at London audiences: 'What's my name? What's my name?' Since nobody could pronounce the squiggle, his demand was greeted with total silence.

5. **ARTHUR LEE.** The frontman of Sixties band Love had a tendency to wander off stage during concerts to go to the supermarket.

6. **SYD BARRETT.** The creative force behind the early days of Pink Floyd has lived as a recluse for years. He has been known to use margarine as hair gel.

7. **OZZY OSBOURNE.** Wild-man of Black Sabbath, he once reputedly bit off a bat's head on stage.

8. **MICHAEL JACKSON.** The operations to have his skin made paler, the mask he wears around his face, the fact that his best friend is a chimpanzee... Enough said.

9. **SKY SAXON.** The singer with cult Californian band The Seeds would wander the streets of Los Angeles in a kaftan asking dogs: 'Pardon me, sir, could you tell me the time?' Also lived in a dustbin like his hero Top Cat.

10. **VIV STANSHALL.** Offstage, the leader of The Bonzo Dog Doo-Dah Band behaved like the archetypal eccentric English aristocrat. On stage, he once put raw meat into Ringo Starr's drum kit (while the Beatles were recording 'Revolver') in a bid to 'foil the Fabs' sound'.

> MUSIC, FILM AND TV

10 ROCK SUICIDES

1. **MICHAEL HOLLIDAY.** The velvet-voiced British crooner shot himself in 1963, seemingly unable to cope with the pressures of fame.

2. **JOE MEEK.** Producer of The Tornados who shot himself on February 3, 1967, the anniversary of the death of his hero, Buddy Holly.

3. **BOBBY BLOOM.** Shot himself in a Hollywood motel room in 1974, although it may have been an accident.

4. **PETE HAM.** One half of Badfinger, he hanged himself in 1975. Tragically, his musical partner, Tom Evans, also committed suicide in 1983.

5. **IAN CURTIS.** The singer with Joy Division hanged himself in 1980.

6. **THE SINGING NUN.** Belgian nun Sister Luc-Gabrielle had a hit in 1963 with 'Dominique' under the name of 'The Singing Nun.' She left the convent in 1967 and reverted to her real name of Janine Deckers. In 1985, she and her companion of ten years Annie Pecher committed suicide, reportedly by downing a massive amount of barbiturates with alcohol.

7. **RICHARD MANUEL.** The pianist with The Band was found hanging in his Florida hotel room in 1986.

8. **ROY BUCHANAN.** The U.S. blues guitarist hanged himself in a prison cell in 1988 following his arrest for drunken behaviour.

9. **DEL SHANNON** was found shot dead in his Californian home in 1990, a .22 rifle by his side.

10. **MICHAEL HUTCHENCE.** The INXS singer was found hanging in a Sydney hotel room in 1997. The coroner's verdict was suicide although rumours were rife that his death was the result of a bizarre sex game which went wrong.

> MUSIC, FILM AND TV

10 EUROVISION SONG CONTEST ROWS

1. The result of the 1969 contest, which ended in a four-way tie between France, Holland, Spain and the UK, caused such a furore that Norway, Sweden, Finland, Portugal and Austria refused to take part the following year.

2. Italy boycotted the 1981 contest, saying that it was too old-fashioned. And France backed out in 1982, French TV chiefs claiming: 'The cost is heavy for small and mediocre results.'

3. Luxembourg snubbed the 1995 contest because, as that year's European City of Culture, they considered it too tacky. Italy also shunned the 1995 event, claiming they couldn't fit it into their TV schedules. Cynics cited Italy's poor record in the contest as a more likely reason.

4. In 1978, Jordanian TV refused to show the Israeli entry on screen. Instead, while Izhar Cohen sang the victorious 'A-Bi-Ni-Bi', Jordanian viewers saw a bunch of flowers. When it seemed likely that Israel were going to win, Jordanian TV switched to an American detective series, *Bronk*. For the 1981 contest in Dublin, Jordan refused to acknowledge the presence of Israel at all, playing commercials and a brief musical interlude while Israel sang. And when voting began, Jordan cut transmission again because the scoreboard showed the name of Israel. Baffled viewers had to wait for another hour until a newsflash informed them that the United Kingdom had won.

5. A diplomatic row erupted in 1987 after BBC presenter Ray Moore light-heartedly referred to the Turkish group Locomotive as 'an ugly crowd.'

6. When Sweden and Norway finished second and third respectively in 1966, the Scandinavians were accused of being partial in their

MUSIC, FILM AND TV

voting. And in 1968, Britain complained that Spain, who won, had deliberately not voted for the UK entry, Cliff Richard's Congratulations', in order to scupper its chances.

7. Dutch members of the audience booed the 1984 UK entry, 'Love Games' by Belle and the Devotions, after newspaper stories in Holland claimed that the song was similar to an old Supremes number.

8. In 1973, Irish singer Maxi threatened to walk out after a row about the arrangement of her song. A substitute singer flew to Luxembourg on stand-by (rehearsing the song on the plane) but Maxi relented and sang on. She came nowhere.

9. Eurovision rules stated that an entry's melody and lyrics must be written by that country's nationals. So when Norway asked French linguistics lecturer Rene Herail to devise a song for the 1982 contest, he got round the loophole by not taking a writing credit for 'Adieu.' The nationality question surfaced again in 1985 when the Luxembourg entry was performed by a six-strong group comprising two Britons, a Canadian, one Dutch, one Belgian and a German.

10. Thirteen-year-old schoolgirl Sandra Kim became the youngest winner when she steered Belgium to victory in 1986. But as a result contestants started to get younger and there was widespread condemnation when, in 1989, France paraded 11-year-old Nathalie Paque and the Israeli singer was a 12-year-old boy called Gili.

The most remarkable story from the chequered 42-year history of the Eurovision Song Contest occurred in 1974 when plotters planning a military coup in Portugal used the playing of the country's Eurovision entry on radio as the signal for tanks to move in.

> MUSIC, FILM AND TV

10 MUSICIANS KILLED IN PLANE CRASHES

1. GLENN MILLER, 1944.
2. BUDDY HOLLY, 1959.
3. PATSY CLINE, 1963.
4. JIM REEVES, 1964.
5. OTIS REDDING, 1967.
6. JIM CROCE, 1973.
7. RONNIE VAN ZANT (Lynyrd Skynyrd), 1977.
8. RICKY NELSON, 1985.
9. KYU SAKAMOTO, 1985.
10. STEVIE RAY VAUGHAN, 1990.

Buddy Holly, Richie Valens and The Big Bopper all died on the same flight from Ohio to Minnesota, a flight they only made because Holly was in a hurry to get to the next gig and to organise clean laundry and get a good night's sleep. Patsy Cline's death was just one link in a chain of tragedy. Cline's plane crashed when she was on her way back to Nashville from Kansas City after giving a benefit concert for the widow of disc jockey Cactus Jack Call who had recently been killed in a car smash. Then, travelling to Cline's funeral, U.S. country star Jack Anglin was also killed in a car crash. Kyu Sakamoto was one of 520 victims when a Japan Airlines 747 crashed near Tokyo. Sakamoto achieved fleeting fame in 1963 with 'Sukiyaki', the only U.S. Number One to be sung entirely in Japanese.

MUSIC, FILM AND TV

APPEARANCES ON OTHER PEOPLE'S RECORDS

1. **RICK WAKEMAN** played synthesizer on David Bowie's "Space Oddity".

2. **MICK JAGGER** sang backing vocals on Carly Simon's "You're So Vain".

3. **ELTON JOHN** played piano on the Hollies' "He Ain't Heavy, He's My Brother".

4. **GEORGE HARRISON** played guitar under the name of L'Angelo Mysterioso on Cream's "Badge".

5. **KATE BUSH** helped out with the vocals on Peter Gabriel's "Games Without Frontiers".

6. **DAVE GILMOUR** played guitar on Kate Bush's "Wuthering Heights".

7. **PHIL COLLINS** played drums on Adam Ant's "Puss 'N Boots".

8. **MICHAEL JACKSON** sang supporting vocals on Rockwell's "Somebody's Watching You".

9. **MARK KING** of Level 42 played bass on Midge Ure's "If I Was".

10. **STEVIE WONDER** played harmonica on Chaka Khan's "I Feel For You"..

Other guest appearances include Eric Clapton playing guitar on the Beatles' "While My Guitar Gently Weeps", Sting supplying high-pitched vocals on Dire Straits' "Money For Nothing" and John Lennon, disguised as Dr. Winston O'Boogie, playing on Elton John's version of "Lucy in the Sky With Diamonds". But one of the most surprising assists was movie star Michael Douglas who sang backing vocals on Billy Ocean's 1986 hit "When The Going Gets Tough (The Tough Get Going)". The song featured in Douglas's movie *The Jewel of the Nile*.

MUSIC, FILM AND TV

20 BEAUTY QUEENS WHO BECAME FILM STARS

1. RAQUEL WELCH (Miss Photogenic 1953).
2. CYBILL SHEPHERD (Miss Teenage Memphis 1966).
3. MICHELLE PFEIFFER (Miss Orange County 1977).
4. YVONNE DE CARLO (Miss Venice Beach 1941).
5. DYAN CANNON (Miss West Seattle 1957).
6. KIM NOVAK (Miss Deepfreeze 1953).
7. JAYNE MANSFIELD (Miss Photoflash 1952).
8. SYLVIA KRISTEL (Miss Television Europe 1973).
9. LAUREN BACALL (Miss Greenwich Village 1942).
10. CLAUDIA CARDINALE (The Most Beautiful Italian Girl in Tunis 1956).
11. DEBBIE REYNOLDS (Miss Burbank 1948).
12. SHIRLEY JONES (Miss Pittsburgh 1951).
13. ANITA EKBERG (Miss Sweden 1951).
14. GINA LOLLOBRIGIDA (Miss Italy 1946).
15. ELKE SOMMER (Miss Viareggio 1959).
16. DOROTHY LAMOUR (Miss New Orleans 1931).
17. SOPHIA LOREN (Princess of the Sea 1948, Miss Elegance 1950).
18. VERONICA LAKE (Miss Florida 1937).
19. VERA MILES (Miss Kansas 1948).
20. ZSA ZSA GABOR (Miss Hungary 1936).

Both Zsa Zsa Gabor and Veronica Lake were subsequently stripped of their titles for being under 16. Michelle Pfeiffer was 18 and working as a supermarket check-out girl, monitoring the price of dog food and packets of washing powder, when her hairdresser suggested she try modelling. She was so bored she gave it a go and rang an agent who entered her in the Miss Orange County contest. She hasn't looked back since.

MUSIC, FILM AND TV

10 FILMS WHICH FEATURE PIGS

1. *Animal Farm (1955)*.

2. *Babe (1995)*.

3. *Big Top Pee Wee (1988)*.

4. *Charlotte's Web (1972)*.

5. *Doc Hollywood (1991)*.

6. *Leon the Pig Farmer (1992)*.

7. *Misery (1990)*.

8. *Pigs (1982)*.

9. *A Private Function (1984)*.

10. *Razorback (1984)*.

MUSIC, FILM AND TV

20 DISNEY VILLAINS

1. CRUELLA DE VIL (*101 Dalmatians*).
2. CAPTAIN HOOK (*Peter Pan*).
3. SHERE KHAN (*The Jungle Book*).
4. STEPMOTHER (*Cinderella*).
5. GASTON (*Beauty and the Beast*).
6. JAFAR (*Aladdin*).
7. MEDUSA (*The Rescuers*).
8. BEAR (*The Fox and the Hound*).
9. QUEEN (*Snow White and the Seven Dwarfs*).
10. STROMBOLI (*Pinocchio*).
11. CHERNOBOG (*Fantasia*).
12. QUEEN OF HEARTS (*Alice in Wonderland*).
13. RAT (*Lady and the Tramp*).
14. MALEFICENT (*Sleeping Beauty*).
15. MADAM MIM (*The Sword in the Stone*).
16. PRINCE JOHN (*Robin Hood*).
17. HORNED KING (*The Black Cauldron*).
18. RATIGAN (*The Great Mouse Detective*).
19. URSULA (*The Little Mermaid*).
20. SCAR (*The Lion King*).

MUSIC, FILM AND TV

20 HOLLYWOOD NICKNAMES

1. **America's Sweetheart — Mary Pickford.**
2. **The Blonde Bombshell — Betty Hutton.**
3. **The Brazilian Bombshell — Carmen Miranda.**
4. **The Duke — John Wayne.**
5. **The Girl with the Million Dollar Legs — Betty Grable.**
6. **The Italian Stallion — Sylvester Stallone.**
7. **The It Girl — Clara Bow.**
8. **The Look — Lauren Bacall.**
9. **The Magnificent Wildcat — Pola Negri.**
10. **The Man of a Thousand Faces — Lon Chaney snr.**
11. **The Meanest Man in the World — Jack Benny.**
12. **The Mexican Spitfire — Lupe Velez.**
13. **The Muscles From Brussels — Jean-Claude Van Damme.**
14. **The Oomph Girl — Ann Sheridan.**
15. **The Platinum Blonde — Jean Harlow.**
16. **The Professional Virgin — Doris Day.**
17. **The Sex Kitten — Brigitte Bardot.**
18. **The Sex Thimble — Dudley Moore.**
19. **The Sweater Girl — Lana Turner.**
20. **The Vagabond Lover — Rudy Vallee.**

Apparently Lupe Velez, Mexican star of the 1940s, was blessed with the ability to rotate her left breast while the other remained motionless. She could also counter-rotate it, a feat which her Australian co-star Leon Erroll described as 'so supple and beautiful you couldn't believe your eyes'.

MUSIC, FILM AND TV

20 ACTORS WHO HAVE CHANGED THEIR NAMES

1. **RED BUTTONS** began life as Aaron Chwatt. The idea for his new identity came from his red hair and the 48 buttons on his bellboy uniform.

2. **MICHAEL CAINE** was born Maurice Micklewhite and took his stage name from an advertisement for the film *The Caine Mutiny*.

3. **GARY COOPER** started out as Frank Cooper but was persuaded to change his name to that of his agent's home town – Gary, Indiana.

4. **MICHAEL CRAWFORD** was known as Michael Dumble-Smith until he took his stage name from a passing Crawford's Biscuits lorry.

5. **BETTE DAVIS** was plain Ruth Davis until she decided to name herself after Balzac's Cousin Bette.

6. **DORIS DAY** scrapped Doris von Kapellof on the advice of bandleader Barney Rapp, for whom she had sung 'Day After Day'.

7. **NICOLAS CAGE** started life as Nicholas Coppola but changed it to distance himself from his uncle, director Francis Ford Coppola. He chose Cage from the comic book character, Luke Cage.

8. **JUDY GARLAND** wisely abandoned Frances Gumm in favour of something more romantic. She borrowed her first name from the Hoagy Carmichael song 'Judy' and took her surname from Chicago theatre critic Robert Garland. The necessity to change her name had been brought about by an early billing which called the 11-year-old 'Frances Glumm'.

9. **CARY GRANT**. The erstwhile Archibald Leach took the name 'Cary' from Cary Lockwood, the character he played in the stage comedy *Nikki*.

MUSIC, FILM AND TV

10. ROCK HUDSON was advised by his agent to change his name from Roy Scherer. The agent consulted an atlas to come up with a compound of the Rock of Gibraltar and New York State's Hudson River.

11. CAROLE LOMBARD, or Jane Peters as she was originally known, adopted her stage name from the Carroll, Lombardi Pharmacy on Lexington and 65th in New York.

12. ZEPPO MARX was christened Herbert Marx but was known as 'Zeppo' because his birth coincided with the first Zeppelin.

13. RAY MILLAND originally used his stepfather's surname, Mullane. Then he suggested 'Mill land' in honour of the beauty of his Welsh homeland.

14. ZERO MOSTEL was born Samuel Joel Mostel but was nicknamed 'Zero' on account of his appalling school grades.

15. LUKE PERRY started out as Coy Luther Perry III but chose Luke from his favourite movie, *Cool Hand Luke*, which he had first seen at the age of five.

16. OMAR SHARIF was Michael Shalhoub until he took 'Omar' from Second World War hero General Omar Bradley and 'Sharif' from the Arab word for nobility, *sherif*.

17. SIGOURNEY WEAVER was born Susan Weaver but chose her distinctive first name from a character in the novel *The Great Gatsby*.

18. OPRAH WINFREY was a mistake. Her name was supposed to be the Biblical 'Orpah' but the midwife spelt it wrongly on the birth certificate.

19. SHELLEY WINTERS was Shirley Schrift but took the name 'Shelley' from the poet.

20. MICHAEL YORK began as Michael Johnson until he took his stage name from York cigarettes.

MUSIC, FILM AND TV

10 BON MOTS FROM WOODY ALLEN

1. 'It's not that I'm afraid to die, I just don't want to be there when it happens' – Allen on death.

2. 'If only God would give me some clear sign! Like making a large deposit in my name at a Swiss bank' – Allen on God.

3. 'That was the most fun I've ever had without laughing' – Allen on sex *(Annie Hall)*.

4. 'Hey, don't knock masturbation! It's sex with someone I love' – Allen on do-it-yourself sex *(Annie Hall)*.

5. 'I don't want to achieve immortality through my work – I want to achieve it through not dying' – Allen on staying alive.

6. 'In Beverly Hills, they don't throw their garbage away. They make it into television shows' – Allen on Hollywood.

7. 'There is the fear that there is an afterlife but no one will know where it's being held' – Allen on life after death.

8. 'I was thrown out of N.Y.U. in my freshman year for cheating on my metaphysics final. You know, I looked within the soul of the boy sitting next to me' – Allen on metaphysics *(Annie Hall)*.

9. 'Money's better than poverty, if only for financial reasons' – Allen on money.

10. 'I'm a practising heterosexual – but bisexuality immediately doubles your chances for a date on Saturday night' – Allen on sexuality.

> MUSIC, FILM AND TV

10 ACTORS WHO HAVE SERVED TIME

1. **BEBE DANIELS** was jailed for ten days in 1921 for speeding. Her next movie, *The Speed Girl*, was about a movie star sent to prison for speeding.

2. **ERROL FLYNN** was imprisoned three times for assault. The final occasion was for hitting a New York cop whom Flynn reckoned had asked for his autograph in a threatening manner.

3. **STACY KEACH** served six months in Reading jail in 1984 for attempting to smuggle $4,500-worth of cocaine into Britain.

4. **SOPHIA LOREN** spent a month in prison in Rome in 1982 for income tax irregularities.

5. **ROBERT MITCHUM** served 59 days in a California jail in 1948 for possessing narcotics.

6. **IVOR NOVELLO** had a month's stay in Wormwood Scrubs after being convicted of obtaining petrol unlawfully during the Second World War.

7. **DUNCAN RENALDO**, the Romanian-born actor who went on to find fame as The Cisco Kid, served eight months in jail for illegal entry to the USA in 1932.

8. **JANE RUSSELL** went to prison in 1978 for drunken driving.

9. **PHIL SILVERS** was sent to reform school in Brooklyn for allegedly attacking his teacher. He claimed self-defence.

10. **MAE WEST** spent two days in jail in 1926 after her Broadway stage show *Sex* was ruled obscene. She received two days' remission for good behaviour.

MUSIC, FILM AND TV

10 FILMS ABOUT BASEBALL

1. *The Babe Ruth Story* (1948), starring William Bendix in the title role. Bendix played baseball for the New York Giants and the New York Yankees and, before turning to acting, played semi-professionally for two years.

2. *The Pride of the Yankees* (1942), starring Gary Cooper as Lou Gehrig.

3. *The Winning Team* (1952) with Ronald Reagan as Grover Cleveland Alexander.

4. *The Pride of St. Louis* (1952), starring Dan Dailey as Dizzy Dean.

5. *Fear Strikes Out* (1957), starring Anthony Perkins as Jim Piersall.

6. *Angels in the Outfield* (1952) – a baseball manager gets help from above. Paul Douglas and Janet Leigh starred.

7. *Take Me Out to the Ball Game* (1949) – a Gene Kelly/Frank Sinatra musical.

8. *Damn Yankees* (1958) – musical starring Gwen Verdon and Tab Hunter.

9. *Bull Durham* (1988) – Kevin Costner (himself a former High School shortstop) starred with Tim Robbins and Susan Sarandon in the tale of minor league baseball team the Durham Bulls.

10. *A League of Their Own* (1992) – Tom Hanks played the team coach in a film set in the 1940s.

MUSIC, FILM AND TV

10 HOLLYWOOD CONTRACTS

1. American actress **MARGUERITE CLARK** had a clause in her contract stating that she would not kiss on screen — on the orders of her husband, Harry Palmerston-Williams, whom she married in 1921. At the time, she was Mary Pickford's principal rival as 'America's sweetheart' but the no-kissing rule ruined her career and she retired in 1921.

2. **CLARA BOW** had it written into her contract with Paramount that none of the crew should use profane language in her presence. In return, Paramount insisted that she remain single and in 1926 offered her a $500,000 bonus on condition that she remained free of scandal during the tenure of the contract. She failed to collect.

3. **EVELYN VENABLE** was another star not permitted to kiss on screen. Her father had a clause to that effect inserted in her 1933 contract with Paramount.

4. **JOAN CRAWFORD**'s 1930 contract with MGM went so far as to specify the hour by which she had to be in bed.

5. A 1931 Warner's contract ordered American actress and boxing fan **VIVIENNE SEGAL** not to yell at prize-fights in case she strained her voice.

6. The contract of **JOE E. BROWN**, the American comedian of the 1930s, forbade him to grow a moustache.

7. **BUSTER KEATON**'s contract with MGM in the 1920s prevented him from smiling on screen.

8. **JOHN BARRYMORE**'s contract said that he never had to be on set before 10.30am.

9. **GEORGE ARLISS**'s contract at Warner in the early 1930s stated that he didn't have to remain on set any later than 4.30pm.

10. **MAURICE CHEVALIER**'s contract with Paramount, signed as talkies were being introduced, was rendered invalid if he ever lost his French accent!

> MUSIC, FILM AND TV

10 ACTORS AND THEIR INSURANCE

1. Boss-eyed BEN TURPIN was insured for $100,000 against the possibility of his eyes ever becoming normal again.

2. In the early 1930s, RKO insured ROSCOE ATES against losing his trademark stutter.

3. When child star SHIRLEY TEMPLE was first insured, her contract stipulated that no money would be paid if the youngster died or suffered injury while drunk.

4. JIMMY 'SCHNOZZLE' DURANTE knew that his bulbous nose was his fortune and accordingly had it insured for $100,000.

5. FRED ASTAIRE had his legs insured for $1,000,000.

6. CHARLIE CHAPLIN insured his famous feet for $150,000.

7. Hollywood heavyweight actor WALTER HIERS took out a $25,000 policy to insure against him losing weight.

8. Glamorous actress KATHLEEN KEY had her neck insured for $25,000.

9. When ANTHONY QUINN had his head shaved for his role as a magician in the 1968 film *The Magus*, he insured against the risk of his hair not growing again afterwards.

10. Irish actress SIOBHAN McKENNA was not exactly renowned for her driving skills. The first time she sat behind the wheel she finished up in a ditch, the second time against a wall and the third time up a tree. Consequently, her insurance policy for the 1964 film *Of Human Bondage* precluded her from driving a car for the duration of the production.

MUSIC, FILM AND TV

10 HOLLYWOOD CHILDHOODS

1. **CLARK GABLE** is listed on his birth certificate as a girl.

2. **JANE SEYMOUR** was born with one green eye and one brown eye.

3. **MARLON BRANDO** used to wander so much on his way to kindergarten that his older sister Jocelyn had to take him to school on a leash.

4. As a child, **ANN-MARGRET**'s family was so poor that they had to live in an Illinois funeral parlour. Every night she slept next to a casket.

5. **DUDLEY MOORE** was born with a club foot. As a result, his left leg was shorter than his right.

6. **CANDICE BERGEN** is the daughter of ventriloquist Edgar Bergen. When she was little, her father's dummy, the inimitable Charlie McCarthy, had a bigger bedroom and more clothes than her.

7. **DEBBIE REYNOLDS** was such a virtuous child that she earned 48 merit badges as a Girl Scout.

8. **RITA HAYWORTH** was born with one eye much larger than the other. She camouflaged it with specially constructed eyelashes.

9. Future Hollywood tough guy **CHARLES BRONSON** had a decidedly non-macho start to life. His family was so poor that he had to wear his sister's hand-me-down dresses to school.

10. **DEMI MOORE** was born cross-eyed.

MUSIC, FILM AND TV

10 SEX CHANGE FILMS

1. *Glen or Glenda?* (1953).

2. *The Christine Jorgensen Story* (1970).

3. *Myra Breckinridge* (1970) where surgeons transformed Rex Reed as movie critic Myron into Raquel Welch as Myra!

4. *Dr. Jekyll and Sister Hyde* (1971).

5. *Dog Day Afternoon* (1975).

6. *Let Me Die a Woman* (1979).

7. *The Woman Inside* (1981).

8. *Come Back to the 5 and Dime, Jimmy Dean, Jimmy Dean* (1982).

9. *Something Special* (1986).

10. *Cleo/Leo* (1989).

> MUSIC, FILM AND TV

10 ACTORS WHO REJECTED STAR ROLES

1. MICHAEL CAINE passed over the Oliver Reed role in the 1969 film *Women in Love* because of the nude wrestling scene with Alan Bates. 'I wouldn't have done it for $20 million,' said Caine.

2. GARY COOPER turned down the role of Rhett Butler in the 1939 epic *Gone With The Wind* because he was convinced it would be a flop. Clark Gable was happy to prove him wrong.

3. JOAN CRAWFORD backed out of the 1953 movie *From Here to Eternity* because she detested the costumes. Deborah Kerr took her place and won an Oscar nomination.

4. HENRY FONDA turned down the role which earned Peter Finch a posthumous Oscar in the 1976 movie *Network* because he considered it to be 'too hysterical'.

5. ANTHONY HOPKINS said 'No' to the part of *Gandhi* (1982) which won Ben Kingsley an Oscar.

6. ANTHONY NEWLEY rejected the title role in the 1966 hit *Alfie* which made Michael Caine a major star.

7. GEORGE RAFT turned down the lead in the 1941 classic *The Maltese Falcon*, allowing Humphrey Bogart to take over.

8. ROBERT REDFORD turned down Dustin Hoffman's role in the 1967 hit *The Graduate*.

9. GEORGE SEGAL quit the 1979 comedy *10* early in filming, enabling Dudley Moore to make his big Hollywood breakthrough.

10. SYLVESTER STALLONE walked out on the 1985 hit *Beverly Hills Cop* when his demand for more action scenes was rejected. Eddie Murphy took over.

MUSIC, FILM AND TV

10 ACTORS WHO HAVE PLAYED MULTIPLE ROLES IN FILMS

1. **ROLF LESLIE** (27 parts in the 1913 life story of Queen Victoria, *Sixty Years a Queen*).
2. **LUPINO LANE** (24 parts in *Only Me*, 1929).
3. **JOSEPH HENABERY** (14 characters in *The Birth of a Nation*, 1915).
4. **ROBERT HIRSCH** (12 roles in *No Questions on Saturday*, 1964).
5. **MICHAEL RIPPER** (9 parts in *What a Crazy World*, 1963).
6. **ALEC GUINNESS** (8 roles in *Kind Hearts and Coronets*, 1949).
7. **JERRY LEWIS** (7 characters in *The Family Jewels*, 1965).
8. **PETER SELLERS** (3 roles in *The Mouse That Roared*, 1959).
9. **TERRY-THOMAS** (3 parts in *Arabella*, 1969).
10. **RED SKELTON** (3 characters in *Watch The Birdie*, 1950).

Peter Sellers revelled in tackling multiple roles. Alec Guinness was his hero and he played three characters in no fewer than three films – *The Mouse That Roared*, *Dr. Strangelove* and *Soft Beds, Hard Battles*. In Stanley Kubrick's *Dr. Strangelove, or How I Learned to Stop Worrying and Love the Bomb*, Sellers played U.S. President Merkin Muffley, RAF Group-Captain Lionel Mandrake and Strangelove himself – a mad Nazi-American inventor with an artificial arm. Kubrick wanted to achieve a 'satiric symmetry' in which 'everywhere you turn there is some version of Peter Sellers holding the fate of the world in his hands.' To this end, Kubrick also wanted Sellers to take on two other roles – Major 'King' Kong and General Buck Turgidson. But when Sellers broke an ankle, Slim Pickens took over as Kong. As for Turgidson, Sellers didn't like the role and thought it was too physically demanding to play yet another character. So George C. Scott stepped in. Incidentally, Sellers based Strangelove's curious little voice on a stills photographer called Weegee.

MUSIC, FILM AND TV

10 SEX SCENE CONFESSIONS

1. 'His idea of a romantic kiss was to go "blaaah" and gag me with his tongue. He only improved once he married Demi Moore' – CYBILL SHEPHERD on BRUCE WILLIS.

2. 'On location it was really uncomfortable. He wasn't a good kisser. Then we came to London and had this great love scene. He was wonderful – I couldn't understand it. It turned out that his wife was with him in London. He was much looser when she was there' – CYBILL SHEPHERD on MICHAEL CAINE in *Silver Bears*.

3. VERONICA LAKE got on so badly with FREDRIC MARCH during *I Married A Witch* that she kneed him in the groin during their love scene.

4. 'I have never considered myself to be a sex symbol. Nobody asked me to do sex scenes – it would only have depressed people' – LAUREN BACALL.

5. 'It was really sexy. I enjoyed bumping up against it even though it had black stuff all over it so that by the end of shooting my face was covered in black goo' – KIM BASINGER being turned on by MICHAEL KEATON's Batman costume.

6. KENNETH WILLIAMS' moment of unbridled passion with JOAN SIMS in *Carry On Up The Khyber* was somewhat marred by Williams' persistent flatulence.

7. 'When I read there was a scene where I had to moon, I thought it was a joke. When I realized it wasn't, I made all the crew moon too so I could look at their ugly bottoms' – EMILY LLOYD on *Wish You Were Here*.

8. LANA TURNER used to chew gum to keep her mouth fresh for screen clinches. CLARK GABLE kissed her so forcibly during *Homecoming* that when they drew back, the pair were attached by a ribbon of sticky gum! From then on, she gargled.

9. 'It's a little too sick, real or feigned, to do it in front of your mother' – JENNIFER JASON LEIGH discussing a sex scene in her 1996 movie *Georgia*, the screenplay for which had been written by her mother, BARBARA TURNER. Leigh asked Turner to leave the set at the crucial moment.

10. 'God, I miss my husband' – PATSY KENSIT's whispered words to MEL GIBSON during their naked romp in *Lethal Weapon 2*.

MUSIC, FILM AND TV

20 HOLLYWOOD INSULTS

1. **JULIE ANDREWS.** 'Working with her is like being hit over the head with a Valentine's card' – **CHRISTOPHER PLUMMER.**

2. **MARLON BRANDO.** 'He has preserved the mentality of an adolescent. When he doesn't try and someone's speaking to him, it's like a blank wall. In fact it's even less interesting because behind a blank wall you can always suppose that there's something interesting there'
– **BURT REYNOLDS.**

3. **RICHARD CHAMBERLAIN.** 'You're doing it the wrong way round, my boy. You're a star and you don't know how to act' – **SIR CEDRIC HARDWICKE.**

4. **JOAN COLLINS.** 'She's common, she can't act – yet she's the hottest female property around these days. If that doesn't tell you something about the state of our industry today, what does?'
– **STEWART GRANGER.**

5. **JOAN CRAWFORD.** 'The best time I ever had with Joan Crawford was when I pushed her down the stairs in *Whatever Happened to Baby Jane?*'
– **BETTE DAVIS.**

6. **GRETA GARBO.** 'Co-starring with Garbo hardly constituted an introduction' – **FREDRIC MARCH.**

7. **RICHARD GERE.** 'I'm always trying to find diplomatic ways to talk about Richard and the movie *An Officer and a Gentleman*. I liked him before we started but that is the last time I can remember talking to him'
– **DEBRA WINGER.**

8. **REX HARRISON.** 'The most brilliant actor that I have ever worked with. I've liked others very much more' – **ANNA NEAGLE.**

9. **JERRY LEWIS.** 'Lewis used to be one of my heroes. When I was a kid, I did pantomimes to his records. He was an enormously talented, phenomenally energetic man who used vulnerability very well. But through the years,

MUSIC, FILM AND TV

I've seen him turn into this arrogant, sour, ceremonial, piously chauvinistic egomaniac' – ELLIOTT GOULD.

10. **SHELLEY LONG.** 'Then there was the question of Shelley's hair (on *Hello Again*). We had to re-shoot the first ten days because it was wrong. All I can say about Shelley is that she is a perfectionist' – GABRIEL BYRNE.

11. **SOPHIA LOREN.** 'I do not talk about Sophia. I do not wish to make for her publicity. She has a talent, but it is not such a big talent' – GINA LOLLOBRIGIDA.

12. **JAYNE MANSFIELD.** 'Dramatic art in her opinion is knowing how to fill a sweater' – BETTE DAVIS.

13. **SARAH MILES.** 'She's a monster. If you think she's not strong, you'd better pay attention' – ROBERT MITCHUM.

14. **STEVE McQUEEN.** 'A Steve McQueen performance just naturally lends itself to monotony. Steve doesn't bring much to the party' – ROBERT MITCHUM.

15. **MARILYN MONROE.** 'It's like kissing Hitler' – TONY CURTIS.

16. **MARGARET O'BRIEN.** 'If that child had been born in the Middle Ages, she'd have been burned as a witch' – LIONEL BARRYMORE.

17. **BARBRA STREISAND.** 'Filming with Streisand is an experience which may have cured me of movies' – KRIS KRISTOFFERSON.

18. **ESTHER WILLIAMS.** 'Wet she's a star. Dry, she ain't' – FANNY BRICE.

19. **MICHAEL WINNER.** 'To say that Michael Winner is his own worst enemy is to provoke a ragged chorus from odd corners of the film industry of "Not while I'm alive"' – BARRY NORMAN.

20. **LORETTA YOUNG.** 'She was and is the only actress I really dislike. She was sickeningly sweet, a pure phoney. Her two faces sent me home angry and crying several times' – VIRGINIA FIELD.

> **MUSIC, FILM AND TV**

10 GUEST VOICES ON THE SIMPSONS

1. LIZ TAYLOR (who gurgled baby Maggie Simpson's first words).
2. MERYL STREEP.
3. MICHELLE PFEIFFER.
4. BOB HOPE.
5. DUSTIN HOFFMAN.
6. MICHAEL JACKSON (as a weirdo).
7. DAVID DUCHOVNY.
8. GILLIAN ANDERSON.
9. PAUL McCARTNEY.
10. AEROSMITH.

MUSIC, FILM AND TV

10 LITTLE KNOWN BATMAN VILLAINS

1. COLONEL GUMM (Roger C. Carmel).

2. DR. CASSANDRA (Ida Lupino).

3. FALSE-FACE (Malachi Throne).

4. LORD FFOGG (Rudy Vallee).

5. MINERVA (Zsa Zsa Gabor).

6. THE MINSTREL (Van Johnson).

7. NORA CLAVICLE (Barbara Rush).

8. SANDMAN (Michael Rennie).

9. THE SIREN (Joan Collins).

10. ZELDA THE GREAT (Anne Baxter).

> **MUSIC, FILM AND TV**

20 CASES OF TV CENSORSHIP

1. The American network banned the words 'breasts' and 'virgin' from *M*A*S*H*. Writer LARRY GELBART got round the ban by inventing a soldier from the Virgin Islands.

2. ELVIS PRESLEY's act was considered so overtly sexual that on America's *Ed Sullivan Show*, he was only filmed from the waist up.

3. In 1966, the BBC tried to postpone an episode of *Pinky and Perky*, entitled 'You Too Can Be a Prime Minister', until after the forthcoming general election lest the programme should contain political bias. There was such an outcry that it was reinstated.

4. 13 episodes of *Upstairs, Downstairs* were banned in the U.S. for 17 years because they dealt with homosexuality and adultery.

5. In the 1950s the BBC banned any jokes about honeymoon couples, chambermaids, fig leaves, lodgers and commercial travellers. Ladies' underwear was another taboo topic. The line 'Winter draws on' was strictly forbidden.

6. The Australian soap *Number 96* contained such risqué bedroom scenes that, for transmission in moralistic Melbourne, a thick black band was superimposed on the bottom half of the screen.

7. Although made in 1978, Roy Minton's Borstal play *Scum*, which contains a vicious rape, was banned from British television until 1991.

8. Dennis Potter's *Brimstone and Treacle*, made in 1976, was not screened in Britain for another 11 years because it dealt with the rape of a handicapped girl.

9. The 1969 drama *Big Breadwinner Hog* (starring PETER EGAN) became the first British programme to be axed in mid-series owing to its violence.

10. For fear of upsetting watchdogs, DICK VAN DYKE and his TV wife MARY TYLER MOORE had to sleep in separate beds on *The Dick Van Dyke Show*.

11. SYLVIA PETERS, the BBC's celebrated announcer of the 1950s, was ordered to wear plastic flowers on the front of her dresses to conceal any hint of cleavage.

MUSIC, FILM AND TV

One evening, after wearing a fashionable strapless evening gown, she was reprimanded by puritanical programme chief Cecil McGivern: 'You looked as if you were appearing in the bath. Please wear a stole in future.'

12. BBC founder LORD REITH once demanded that the statue of Prospero and Ariel, which graces the entrance of Broadcasting House, be taken down so that the size of their genitals could be reduced.

13. LUCILLE BALL was never allowed to say 'pregnant' on *I Love Lucy*. It had to be 'expecting'.

14. An episode of MICHAEL BENTINE's *It's a Square World*, in which a Chinese junk sank the House of Commons, was banned by the BBC until after an approaching general election. A baffled Bentine commented: 'Apparently, there is a BBC edict that you must show parity to the parties at election time. I would have imagined that if you sank the Commons you were showing parity to everybody!'

15. Produced in 1966, PETER WATKINS' drama *The War Game*, about a hypothetical nuclear attack on Britain, was banned until 1985 because it was thought that it would frighten elderly people to death.

16. In 1997, Channel 4's *The Big Breakfast* banned All Saints' singer MELANIE BLATT from appearing live on the programme for six months after she swore on-air.

17. Dancer KERRY MARTIN was sacked from the BBC's Fifties pop show *Six-Five Special* for wiggling too much during a routine.

18. A full-frontal male nude and actress GEMMA CRAVEN's nipples were censored from Dennis Potter's *Pennies From Heaven*.

19. American network ABC refused to let a fully-dressed Jeff Colby kiss wife Fallon's foot in *The Colbys* for fear of encouraging foot-fetishists.

20. In 1961, Granada prepared a documentary on television censorship. It was banned.

MUSIC, FILM AND TV

10 DEFECTIVE DETECTIVES

1. **MARK SABER** — one arm.

2. **COLONEL MARCH** — one eye.

3. **MIKE LONGSTREET** — blind.

4. **CHIEF ROBERT T. IRONSIDE** — wheelchair-bound.

5. **COLUMBO** — no dress sense.

6. **FRANK CANNON** — obese.

7. **THEO KOJAK** — bald.

8. **JIM BERGERAC** — ex-alcoholic with dodgy leg.

9. **JIM ROCKFORD** — ex-con.

10. **EDDIE SHOESTRING** — ex-nervous breakdown.

MUSIC, FILM AND TV

10 U.S. DETECTIVE SHOWS NOT SET IN LOS ANGELES

1. HOMICIDE — LIFE ON THE STREET (Baltimore).

2. THE STREETS OF SAN FRANCISCO (San Francisco).

3. N.Y.P.D. BLUE (New York).

4. MIAMI VICE (Miami).

5. FATHER DOWLING INVESTIGATES (Chicago).

6. BANACEK (Boston).

7. HAWAII FIVE-O (Hawaii).

8. McCLOUD (New York).

9. VEGA$ (Las Vegas).

10. McMILLAN AND WIFE (San Francisco).

THE WORLD ABOUT US

20 DREAMS AND THEIR SEXUAL CONNOTATIONS

1. AEROPLANE (penis).
2. BOTTLE (vagina).
3. DART (sexual penetration).
4. DOME (woman's breast).
5. FAIRIES (the feminine side of a man's personality).
6. FIG (testicles).
7. FROG (male genitals).
8. GOAT (male sexuality).
9. GUN (penis).
10. HARBOUR (womb).
11. LOCOMOTIVE GOING INTO TUNNEL (sexual intercourse).
12. MERMAID (fear of frigidity in a woman).
13. MOUNTING A HORSE (sex act).
14. NOSEBLEED (female genitalia).
15. ROLLER-COASTER (sex act).
16. SWEETS (sexual pleasures).
17. SWINGS (desire).
18. VALLEY (hollow in woman's body between breasts or thighs).
19. WATER-LILY (vagina).
20. WOLF (repressed sexual urges).

Apparently the wolf in 'Little Red Riding Hood' represents an inexperienced woman's fear of sexual contact with a man. In its earliest forms, the story is thought to have acted as a warning to young girls against sleeping with men. Freud also claimed that the story of 'The Frog Prince' (in which a girl's embrace transforms a frog into a handsome prince) represents a virgin overcoming her sexual fear.

> THE WORLD ABOUT US

10 NATIONAL SUPERSTITIONS

1. **CHINA:** Sweeping out a house removes all the good luck, especially on Chinese New Year.

2. **HOLLAND:** People with red hair bring bad luck.

3. **IBIZA:** It is bad luck to allow a priest on a fishing boat.

4. **ICELAND:** An unmarried person who sits at the corner of a table won't marry for seven years. A pregnant woman who drinks from a cracked cup risks having a baby with a hare-lip.

5. **IRELAND:** It is unlucky to use broken tombstones for the walls of a cottage. It is lucky to spill drink on the ground.

6. **JAPAN:** Picking up a comb with its teeth facing your body brings bad luck.

7. **MALTA:** Churches with two towers are fitted with a clock face in each but the two clocks always tell different times to confuse the Devil about the time of the service.

8. **NIGERIA:** A man hit with a broom becomes impotent unless he retaliates seven times with the same broom. Sweeping a house at night brings misfortune to the occupants.

9. **POLAND:** Bringing lilac into the house is a sure sign of impending death.

10. **SCOTLAND:** Red and green should never be worn together. It is unlucky to throw vegetables on to the fire and to carry a spade through the house. This means that a grave will soon be dug. And three swans flying together means a national disaster is imminent.

> THE WORLD ABOUT US

10 UNUSUAL FESTIVALS

1. CHEESE-ROLLING (U.K., May). Cheese-rolling has taken place on the 1 in 2 slopes of Cooper's Hill, near Birdlip in Gloucestershire, since the 15th Century. At 6pm on Spring Bank Holiday Monday, local youths line up at the top of the hill alongside a 7lb circular Double Gloucester cheese. When the cheese is released, the competitors hurtle down the hill in an attempt to catch it before it reaches the bottom. Eight people were injured during the 1992 event.

2. DAY OF THE DEAD (Mexico, November 2). According to Indian folklore, this is the day when the deceased return to life. Families conduct macabre graveside picnics, offering food to the dead, and then tuck into a feast of their own, eating chocolate coffins, sugar wreaths and fancy breads adorned with skulls and crossbones.

3. DOO DAH PARADE (U.S., Thanksgiving). A spoof version of the glittering Rose Parade held each year in Pasadena, California, the Doo Dah Parade has deliberately become a byword in tackiness with badly-decorated floats, inept drill teams and a routine where businessmen in suits perform with their briefcases.

4. GOTMAAR FESTIVAL (India, September). On the day following the September full moon, the 45,000 inhabitants of Pandhura divide themselves into two groups and start hurling rocks at each other until sunset when the fighting ends. The festivities can get out of hand. In 1989 there were 616 casualties, including four deaths.

5. GRANDMOTHERS' FESTIVAL (Norway, July). First held at Bodo in 1992, the festival sees grannies riding motorbikes, racehorses, skydiving and scuba-diving. The star of the inaugural event was 79-year-old Elida Anderson who became the world's oldest bungee-jumper.

THE WORLD ABOUT US

6. KING OF THE MOUNTAIN FESTIVAL (Australia, October). With a summit just 140ft above the surrounding plains, Mount Wycheproof in Victoria is registered as the lowest mountain in the world. This fact is celebrated annually with a foot-race up the mountain with each contestant carrying a sack of wheat weighing 140 lb.

7. LA TOMATINA (Spain). This festival dates back to 1944 when the fair at Buñol was ruined by hooligans hurling tomatoes at the procession. Now each year the town stages a 90-minute mass fight with 190,000lb of ripe tomatoes, an event which has relegated the annual fair to the status of a mere sideshow.

8. MOOSE-DROPPING FESTIVAL (Alaska, July). The town of Talkeetna plays host to an annual celebration of moose-droppings. Stalls sell jewellery and assorted knick-knacks made from moose-droppings but pride of place goes to the moose-dropping-throwing competition where competitors toss gold-painted moose-droppings into a target area, the winner being the one who lands his dropping closest to the centre target.

9. RUNNING OF THE SHEEP (U.S., September). Reedpoint, Montana, stages a gentle alternative to Spain's famous Running of the Bulls. Each September hundreds of sheep charge down Main Street for six blocks. Contests are held for the ugliest sheep and prettiest ewe while shepherds assemble to recite poetry.

10. SWINGING THE FIREBALLS (Scotland, New Year's Eve). Residents of Stonehaven march through the town swinging great balls of fire made from wire netting and filled with driftwood, pine cones, twigs and oil-soaked rags. The balls are then thrown into the harbour to herald the New Year. The ceremony is thought to date back to the Middle Ages when the towns-folk tried to charm the sun from the heavens during the long, cold winter months.

> **THE WORLD ABOUT US**

THE NICKNAMES OF 20 U.S. STATES

1. ALABAMA — Cotton State.
2. ARKANSAS — Bear State.
3. CONNECTICUT — Nutmeg State.
4. DELAWARE — Diamond State.
5. FLORIDA — Sunshine State.
6. INDIANA — Hoosier State.
7. IOWA — Hawkeye State.
8. KENTUCKY — Bluegrass State.
9. LOUISIANA — Pelican State (a pelican features on the coat of arms).
10. MICHIGAN — Wolverine State.
11. MINNESOTA — Gopher State.
12. MISSISSIPPI — Magnolia State.
13. MISSOURI — Show Me State.
14. NEW HAMPSHIRE — Granite State.
15. NORTH CAROLINA — Tar Heel State.
16. NORTH DAKOTA — Flickertail State (for its large population of squirrels).
17. OHIO — Buckeye State (for the trees that grow there).
18. OREGON — Beaver State.
19. UTAH — Beehive State.
20. WISCONSIN — Badger State (because Wisconsin miners are believed to have made homes by burrowing underground).

THE WORLD ABOUT US

10 COMMENTS ABOUT AMERICANS

1. I am willing to love all mankind, except an American — DR. SAMUEL JOHNSON.

2. It was wonderful to find America, but it would have been more wonderful to miss it — MARK TWAIN.

3. The American male doesn't mature until he has exhausted all other possibilities — U.S. writer WILFRED SHEED.

4. Of course, America had often been discovered before Columbus, but it had always been hushed up — OSCAR WILDE.

5. America is the only nation in history which, miraculously, has gone directly from barbarism to degeneration without the usual interval of civilisation — former French Prime Minister GEORGES CLEMENCEAU.

6. No one can be as calculatedly rude as the British, which amazes Americans, who do not understand studied insult and can only offer abuse as a substitute — PAUL GALLICO.

7. America is the country where you buy a lifetime supply of aspirin for one dollar, and use it up in two weeks — JOHN BARRYMORE.

8. If you're going to America, bring your own food — U.S. writer FRAN LEBOWITZ.

9. The trouble with America is that there are far too many wide open spaces surrounded by teeth — U.S. writer CHARLES LUCKMAN.

10. The 100% American is 99% idiot — GEORGE BERNARD SHAW.

THE WORLD ABOUT US

THE 20 LARGEST AMERICAN STATES (AREA IN SQ. KM.).

1. ALASKA (1,531,100).
2. TEXAS (691,200).
3. CALIFORNIA (411,100).
4. MONTANA (381,200).
5. NEW MEXICO (315,000).
6. ARIZONA (294,100).
7. NEVADA (286,400).
8. COLORADO (269,700).
9. WYOMING (253,400).
10. OREGON (251,500).
11. UTAH (219,900).
12. MINNESOTA (218,700).
13. IDAHO (216,500).
14. KANSAS (213,200).
15. NEBRASKA (200,400).
16. SOUTH DAKOTA (199,800).
17. NORTH DAKOTA (183,100).
18. OKLAHOMA (181,100).
19. MISSOURI (180,600).
20. WASHINGTON (176,700).

THE WORLD ABOUT US

THE 20 SMALLEST AMERICAN STATES (AREA IN SQ. KM.).

1. DISTRICT OF COLUMBIA (180).
2. RHODE ISLAND (3,100).
3. DELAWARE (5,300).
4. CONNECTICUT (13,000).
5. HAWAII (16,800).
6. NEW JERSEY (20,200).
7. MASSACHUSETTS (21,500).
8. NEW HAMPSHIRE (24,000).
9. VERMONT (24,900).
10. MARYLAND (31,600).
11. WEST VIRGINIA (62,900).
12. SOUTH CAROLINA (80,600).
13. MAINE (86,200).
14. INDIANA (93,700).
15. KENTUCKY (104,700).
16. VIRGINIA (105,600).
17. OHIO (107,100).
18. TENNESSEE (109,200).
19. PENNSYLVANIA (117,400).
20. MISSISSIPPI (123,600)

THE WORLD ABOUT US

20 FOREIGN CURRENCIES YOU MAY NOT HAVE COME ACROSS

1. Aht (THAILAND).
2. Colón (COSTA RICA).
3. Dalasi (GAMBIA).
4. Dong (VIETNAM).
5. Goude (HAITI).
6. Guarani (PARAGUAY).
7. Kina (PAPUA NEW GUINEA).
8. Kwanza (ANGOLA).
9. Lempira (HONDURAS).
10. Lilangeni (SWAZILAND).
11. New Kip (LAOS).
12. Ngultrum (BHUTAN).
13. Ougiya (MAURETANIA).
14. Pataca (MACAO).
15. Pula (BOTSWANA).
16. Quetzal (GUATEMALA).
17. Riel (CAMBODIA).
18. Taka (BANGLADESH).
19. Tugrik (MONGOLIA).
20. Won (NORTH KOREA).

Cheese was once a form of currency in some European countries. In 16th-century Denmark it was used to pay church taxes, while in the 12th century Blanche of Navarre tried to win the heart of French King Philippe Auguste by sending him 200 cheeses each year.

10 COCA COLA SLOGANS

1. **DELICIOUS! REFRESHING! EXHILARATING! INVIGORATING! (1886).**
2. **THE PAUSE THAT REFRESHES (1929).**
3. **IT'S THE REFRESHING THING TO DO (1936).**
4. **IT'S THE REAL THING (1942, revived in 1969).**
5. **GLOBAL HIGH SIGN (1944).**
6. **THINGS GO BETTER WITH COKE (1963).**
7. **HAVE A COKE AND A SMILE (1979).**
8. **COKE IS IT (1982).**
9. **YOU CAN'T BEAT THE FEELING (1987).**
10. **ALWAYS (1993).**

Originally concocted by Atlanta pharmacist John Styth Pemberton as a headache cure, Coca-Cola proved a popular thirst-quencher with the addition of soda. Unfortunately, Pemberton was a poor salesman, and shortly before his death in 1888 he sold the secret formula plus his share in Coca-Cola to businessman Asa G. Candler for $1,200. Thirty years later, Candler too sold the company...for $25 million. The formula remains a closely-guarded secret, but in 1985 Coca-Cola announced that after 99 years it was abandoning the Pemberton formula in favour of a supposedly new improved taste called 'New Coke'. 'The best has been made even better' proclaimed company chairman Roberto Goizueta. Before taking this momentous decision, Coca-Cola spent $4 million and two years of market research. Yet within three months public pressure forced the company to admit that it had made a mistake and was bringing back the old Coke under the name 'Coca-Cola Classic'.

THE WORLD ABOUT US

10 PLACES WHERE UFOS HAVE BEEN REPORTED

1. **ASHLAND, NEBRASKA.** Police patrolman Herbert Schirmer said he was on patrol in the early hours of December 3, 1967 when he came across a flying saucer. He went on to state under hypnosis that he had been abducted by the alien occupants whom he described as being just under 5ft tall with big chests, thin heads, cat-like eyes and 'funny-looking' lips. They were dressed in one-piece silver suits with no zips. He said that he asked the aliens whether they had kidnapped people and was told that there was 'a breeding analysis programme' involving some humans. He didn't pursue this line of questioning in case he too was kidnapped.

2. **BLACKFORD COUNTY, INDIANA.** De Wayne Donathan and his wife were driving home early one evening in October 1973 when they spotted a tractor-like vehicle parked by the side of the road. As they got nearer, they saw two silver-suited figures dancing. The Donathans drove past and when they turned round the figures had disappeared, but two separate bright lights were flickering in the sky.

3. **DRAKENSBERG MOUNTAINS, SOUTH AFRICA.** In the spring of 1951, a driver was stopped late at night by a short man with a domed, bald head and a strange voice who said he needed water. The witness took the water to a disc-shaped craft and was invited inside where he met a second alien. When asked where they came from, the entities pointed at the sky and said: 'From there'.

4. **KAIKOURA, NEW ZEALAND.** On December 21, 1978, Captains Verne Powell and John Randle were flying from Blenheim to Christchurch when they saw several radar and visual sightings of UFOs. At one point, there were five strong radar targets where none should have been. Ten days later, Channel O from Melbourne retraced the flight and filmed a mysterious object with a flashing light. Its identity remains a mystery.

5. **LIVINGSTON, SCOTLAND.** On November 9, 1979, forester Robert Taylor was confronted by a large, globe-shaped craft hovering above the ground. Suddenly, two spherical, mine-like objects rushed towards him, grabbed him by the legs and dragged him towards the craft. The choking smell caused him to pass out. When he awoke, his trousers were torn and the craft had gone. He couldn't walk or talk properly and had a raging thirst for two days.

THE WORLD ABOUT US

6. NEW YORK STATE. After watching UFOs on the evening of May 2, 1968, Shane Kurz fell asleep. When she woke, muddy footprints led into the house from outside. Years later under regression hypnosis she recalled being drawn to the window by a telepathic voice calling to her. She then went to a UFO in a muddy field where she was taken inside the craft and raped by the alien leader.

7. PALOMOR GARDENS, CALIFORNIA. George Adamski claimed he regularly spoke to aliens, his first encounter being in the Californian desert on November 20, 1952. Apparently the two communicated in sign language and telepathy, the alien indicating that he came from Venus. Adamski went on to claim that he had often travelled in flying saucers, in the course of which he also met Martians and Saturnians.

8. VALENSOLE, FRANCE. On July 1, 1965, farmer Maurice Masse saw a six-legged, egg-shaped UFO in his lavender field. Two entities emerged, wearing green ski suits. They were 4ft tall with large bald heads, big eyes and no lips and they made strange gutteral sounds. One pointed a rod at Masse, immobilising him. After the close encounter, no lavender plants would grow on the landing site for ten years.

9. VILVORDE, BELGIUM. On December 19, 1973, a man went into his kitchen in the middle of the night and saw a 3ft-tall green humanoid glowing in his garden. It had pointed ears and big yellow oval eyes. After a few moments, it made a V-sign before walking up and over the garden wall. The witness calmly went on to make a snack.

10. WEXFORD, REPUBLIC OF IRELAND. Two teenage boys were out walking one evening in September 1924 when they encountered a solid beam of light, several feet long, travelling through the air a few feet off the ground. It climbed over a hedge and across a field until it met a railway line and moved off, following the track. The boys maintained that they saw the object for a good five minutes.

THE WORLD ABOUT US

THE MEANINGS BEHIND 20 CAPITAL CITIES

1. **ADDIS ABABA (Ethiopia)** — new flower.
2. **ALGIERS (Algeria)** — the islands.
3. **BAGHDAD (Iraq)** — God's gift.
4. **BANGKOK (Thailand)** — wild plum village.
5. **BEIJING (China)** — northern capital.
6. **BRUSSELS (Belgium)** — buildings on a marsh.
7. **BUENOS AIRES (Argentina)** — good winds.
8. **CAIRO (Egypt)** — victorious.
9. **CANBERRA (Australia)** — meeting-place.
10. **COPENHAGEN (Denmark)** — merchants' harbour.
11. **DELHI (India)** — threshold.
12. **DUBLIN (Republic of Ireland)** — black pool or lake.
13. **JAKARTA (Indonesia)** — place of victory.
14. **KHARTOUM (Sudan)** — elephant's trunk.
15. **KUALA LUMPUR (Malaysia)** — mud-yellow estuary.
16. **KUWAIT CITY (Kuwait)** — enclosed.
17. **MONTEVIDEO (Uruguay)** — I saw the mountain.
18. **RANGOON (Myanmar)** — end of strife.
19. **SAN SALVADOR (Salvador)** — holy saviour.
20. **TEHRAN (Iran)** — warm place.

THE WORLD ABOUT US

10 COUNTRIES' FORMER NAMES

1. BELIZE (British Honduras).
2. BOTSWANA (Bechuanaland).
3. BURKINA FASO (Upper Volta).
4. CAMBODIA (Kampuchea).
5. ETHIOPIA (Abyssinia).
6. IRAN (Persia).
7. MALAWI (Nyasaland).
8. SRI LANKA (Ceylon).
9. TANZANIA (Tanganyika).
10. DEMOCRATIC REPUBLIC OF THE CONGO (Belgian Congo/Zaire).

> THE WORLD ABOUT US

THE WORLD'S 10 LARGEST ISLANDS (AREA IN SQ KM)

1. AUSTRALIA (7,892,300).
2. GREENLAND (2,131,600).
3. NEW GUINEA (790,000).
4. BORNEO (737,000).
5. MADAGASCAR (587,000).
6. BAFFIN (507,000).
7. SUMATRA (425,000).
8. HONSHU (Hondo) (228,000).
9. GREAT BRITAIN (219,000).
10. VICTORIA, Canada (217,300).

> THE WORLD ABOUT US

THE WORLD'S 10 HIGHEST WATERFALLS (IN METRES)

1. **ANGEL (upper fall), Venezuela (807).**

2. **ITATINGA, Brazil (628).**

3. **CUQUENAN, Guyana/Venezuela (610).**

4. **ORMELI, Norway (563).**

5. **TYSEE, Norway (533).**

6. **PILAO, Brazil (524).**

7. **RIBBON, U.S.A. (491).**

8. **VESTRE MARDOLA, Norway (468).**

9. **RORAIMA, Guyana (457).**

10. **CLEVE-GARTH, New Zealand (450).**

> THE WORLD ABOUT US

THE WORLD'S 10 LONGEST RIVERS (LENGTH IN KM)

1. NILE (North-East Africa) (6,695).

2. AMAZON (South America) (6,516).

3. CHANG JIANG (China) (6,380).

4. MISSISSIPPI-MISSOURI (U.S.A.) (6,019).

5. OB-IRTYSH (Russia) (5,570).

6. YENISEI-ANGARA (Russia) (5,550).

7. YELLOW RIVER (Huang He) (China) (5,464).

8. ZAIRE (D.R. Congo) (4,667).

9. MEKONG (Asia) (4,425).

10. AMUR (Russia) (4,416).

THE WORLD ABOUT US

20 LOST DISTILLERIES OF SCOTLAND

1. **ARDGOWAN**, Greenock (1896–1952).
2. **ARDLUSSA**, Campbeltown (1879–1923).
3. **AUCHINBLAE**, Kincardineshire (1896–1926).
4. **BON ACCORD**, Aberdeen (1855–1910).
5. **BONNINGTON**, Edinburgh (1798–1853).
6. **DALARUAN**, Campbeltown (1824–1922).
7. **DEAN**, Edinburgh (1881–1922).
8. **DRUMCALDIE**, Windygates, Fife (1896–1903).
9. **GLEN ALBYN**, Inverness (1846–1986).
10. **GLEN CAWDOR**, Nairn (1898–1927).
11. **GLENCOULL**, Angus (1897–1929).
12. **GLENMAVIS**, Bathgate (1795–1910).
13. **GLENSKIACH**, Easter Ross (1896–1926).
14. **GLENUGIE**, near Peterhead (1821–1983).
15. **GRANGE**, Burntisland (1795–1925).
16. **LANGHOLM**, Dumfriesshire (1765–1921).
17. **LOCHINDAAL**, island of Islay (1829–1929).
18. **MAN O'HOY**, Stromness, Orkney (1817–1928).
19. **RIECLACHAN**, Campbeltown (1825–1934).
20. **YOKER**, Glasgow (1770–1928).

The isolated settlement of Campbeltown near the Mull of Kintyre used to be the whisky capital of Scotland. No fewer than 33 distilleries were founded in the town, and major customers including the German army... until 1914. By the end of the First World War, 20 distilleries were still going strong but the closure of the local coal mine in 1923 brought an end to cheap fuel supplies and when the railway also shut around 1930, there were only three distilleries working. Now there are just two — Glen Scotia and Springbank.

THE WORLD ABOUT US

10 FOREIGN NAMES FOR COLONEL MUSTARD

1. **COLONEL MOUTARDE** (Belgium, France).
2. **KOLONEL MUSTARD** (Netherlands).
3. **OBERST VON GATOW** (Germany).
4. **MADAME CURRY** (Switzerland).
5. **MARQUÉS DE MARINA** (Spain).
6. **CORONEL MONTEIRO** (Portugal).
7. **SI. MUSTARDAS** (Greece).
8. **ÖVERSTE SENAP** (Sweden, Finland, Denmark).
9. **OBERST GULIN** (Norway).
10. **COLONELLO MUSTARD** (Italy).

The thought of Colonel Mustard swapping his tweeds and army boots for a floral dress and stilettos every time he ventures to Switzerland is mind-boggling. But he is not the only Cluedo participant to use an alias when travelling abroad. In France, the Rev. Green is known as Dr. Olive; Miss Scarlett calls herself Fröken Röd in Scandinavia; Mrs. Peacock becomes the romantic Dona Violeta in Brazil; and in the same country the chameleon-like Professor Plum changes to Professor Black. Meanwhile in the United States, the perpetual victim, Dr. Black, is known as Mr. Boddy. Cluedo was devised by English solicitor's clerk Anthony E. Pratt in 1944. Mr. Pratt, who described himself as 'an introvert full of ruminations, speculations and imaginative notions', teamed up with his wife, an amateur artist. She did the drawings and it is on the board which she designed that the game is still played today. With six characters, six weapons and nine rooms, there are a potential 324 different murder combinations. Cluedo went on sale in 1949 and has since been sold in some 75 countries. It has been calculated that enough rope has been included in these sets to encircle the world.

> THE WORLD ABOUT US

20 LITTLE KNOWN INVENTORS

1. GEORGE C. BEIDLER, American inventor of the photocopier, 1903.
2. HARRY BREARLEY, English inventor of stainless steel, 1913.
3. WILLIS CARRIER, American inventor of air-conditioning, 1902.
4. GEORGES CLAUDE, French inventor of neon lighting, 1910.
5. MRS. W.A. COCHRAN, American inventor of the automatic dishwasher, 1889.
6. ADOLPH E. FICK, German inventor of contact lenses, 1887.
7. DR. R.N. HARGER, American inventor of the breathalyser (or 'drunkometer' as it was then known), 1938.
8. EDWIN T. HOLMES, American inventor of the burglar alarm, 1858.
9. MILLER REESE HUTCHINSON, American inventor of the hearing-aid, 1901.
10. WHITCOMB L. JUDSON, American inventor of the zip, 1893.
11. CARLTON C. MAGEE, American inventor of the parking meter, 1935.
12. JACK MARKS, English inventor of the boxer's gumshield, 1902.
13. KARL LUDWIG NESSLER, German inventor of the hair perm, 1906. He only became a hairdresser because his eyesight was too poor for shoemaking.
14. JAMES RANSOME, English inventor of the motor mower, 1902.
15. ERIK ROTHEIM, Norwegian inventor of the aerosol, 1926.
16. LUCIEN B. SMITH, American inventor of barbed wire, 1874.
17. CHARLES STRITE, American inventor of the pop-up toaster, 1927.
18. JOHANN VAALER, Norwegian inventor of the paper clip, 1900.
19. ARTHUR WYNNE, English inventor of the crossword, 1913.
20. JOSEPH L. ZIMMERMAN, American inventor of the telephone answering machine, 1949. His first device was called the Electronic Secretary.

THE WORLD ABOUT US

10 TRADE NAMES THAT HAVE ENTERED THE ENGLISH LANGUAGE

1. BIRO.
2. ESCALATOR.
3. HOOVER.
4. JACUZZI.
5. LINOLEUM.
6. PLASTICINE.
7. SELLOTAPE.
8. THERMOS.
9. VASELINE.
10. XEROX.

The biro was the brainchild of Hungarian hypnotist, sculptor and journalist Laszlo Biro. In 1938 he was editing a government-sponsored magazine and, on a trip to the printers in Budapest, began considering the virtues of transferring the printers' quick-drying ink to pens. Biro produced a patent for his pen, which featured a rotating steel ball-point, in 1943, around which time he met Englishman Henry Martin, a government employee who recognized the potential of the new pen in wartime. It didn't leak at any altitude (making it ideal for aircrew), it was able to write on damp paper and at awkward angles and could write 200,000 words without refilling. Martin acquired the U.K. rights from Biro and in 1944 began producing ball-point pens for the RAF. Biro not only lost out in Britain but he also forgot to patent his invention in the United States. It was a costly lapse since Gimkel's of New York sold 10,000 at $12.50 apiece on the first day of sale in 1945.

THE WORLD ABOUT US

10 CONDOM BRAND NAMES

1. BILLY BOY (Germany).
2. ENORMEX (U.K.).
3. EUROGLIDER (Netherlands).
4. HAPPY FACE (New Zealand).
5. HONEYMOON SUPER STIMULATION (Germany).
6. JIFFI EXCITER (U.K.).
7. LICKS (U.S.A.).
8. MAMBA (Sweden).
9. POWER PLAY (U.S.A.).
10. SKIN LESS SKIN (Japan).

Italian anatomist Gabrielle Fallopius published the first known description of a condom in 1564. It was made from linen but most early condoms were of animal intestines, soaked before use. Since they were porous, people were advised to wear two at a time — one on top of the other. Casanova used condoms made from the dried gut of a sheep while the Japanese preferred condoms made from tortoiseshell, presumably to slow things down. The vulcanisation of rubber brought about a new material and the brand Durex, much to the confusion of Australians to whom sellotape is known as Durex. Japan uses more condoms than any other country — they are sold door-to-door by 'skin ladies' — and the Tokyo head office of manufacturer Fuji Latex is built in the shape of a condom. Sweden has its own official penis character, Proud Pete, to encourage the use of condoms while some Danish restaurants began serving after-dinner condoms instead of mints. Flavours include banana, lemon, liquorice, mint, strawberry, Caribbean coconut and peach punch. There are condoms that glow in the dark and musical condoms. Italian physics student Lino Missio has patented a condom with a microchip which warns of any tear during sex by playing a Beethoven theme.

THE WORLD ABOUT US

20 CARS WHICH ARE NAMED AFTER PEOPLE

1. **ALFA-ROMEO** (Nicola Romeo — the 'Alfa' stood for Anonima Lombarda Fabbrica Automobili, or Lombardy Automobile Works Company).
2. **ASTON MARTIN** (Lionel Martin who won races on Aston Clinton hill, near Aylesbury).
3. **BUGATTI** (Ettore Bugatti).
4. **CHEVROLET** (Louis Chevrolet).
5. **CHRYSLER** (Walter Percy Chrysler).
6. **CITROËN** (André-Gustave Citröen).
7. **DAIMLER** (Gottfried Daimler).
8. **FERRARI** (Enzo Ferrari).
9. **HILLMAN** (William Hillman).
10. **HONDA** (Soichiro Honda).
11. **LANCIA** (Vincenzo Lancia).
12. **MASERATI** (Maserati brothers — Carlo, Bindo, Alfieri, Ettore and Ernesto).
13. **MERCEDES** (Mercedes Jellinek, the ten-year-old daughter of Austrian financier and motor-racing enthusiast Emil Jellinek).
14. **OPEL** (Adam Opel).
15. **PEUGEOT** (Armand Peugeot).
16. **PORSCHE** (Ferdinand Porsche).
17. **ROLLS-ROYCE** (Charles Rolls and Henry Royce).
18. **SKODA** (Emil Skoda).
19. **TOYOTA** (Sakichi Toyoda — the family changed the name to Toyota since 'Toyoda' needs ten characters in Japanese but 'Toyota' only eight. And eight is the Japanese lucky number).
20. **VANWALL** (Tony Vandervell).

> THE WORLD ABOUT US

20 FAMOUS OWNERS OF LAND ROVERS

1. BRYAN ADAMS.
2. JIM CARREY.
3. FIDEL CASTRO.
4. SEAN CONNERY.
5. KEVIN COSTNER.
6. TOM CRUISE.
7. MICHAEL DOUGLAS.
8. JANE FONDA.
9. MICHAEL J. FOX.
10. MEL GIBSON.
11. JANET JACKSON.
12. MICHAEL JORDAN.
13. BILL MURRAY.
14. JACK NICHOLSON.
15. ROSS PEROT.
16. MEG RYAN.
17. STING.
18. PATRICK SWAYZE.
19. ROBIN WILLIAMS.
20. OPRAH WINFREY.

THE WORLD ABOUT US

20 FAMOUS HARLEY-DAVIDSON OWNERS

1. MUHAMMAD ALI.
2. ANN-MARGRET.
3. CHER.
4. ERIC CLAPTON.
5. DAVID COPPERFIELD.
6. JACK DEMPSEY.
7. NEIL DIAMOND.
8. CLINT EASTWOOD.
9. CLARK GABLE.
10. GOLDIE HAWN.
11. BILLY JOEL.
12. DON JOHNSON.
13. CHARLES LINDBERGH.
14. GEORGE MICHAEL.
15. CROWN PRINCE OLAF OF NORWAY.
16. OLIVIA NEWTON-JOHN.
17. PRISCILLA PRESLEY.
18. LOU REED.
19. BARBRA STREISAND.
10. LIZ TAYLOR.

Created by William S. Harley and Arthur Davidson in a small shed in Milwaukee in 1903, the Harley-Davidson has become a celebrity status symbol, its popularity confirmed by films such as *Easy Rider*. Dan Aykroyd, star of *The Blues Brothers*, is another celebrated HD owner and led John Belushi's funeral procession on a Harley.

THE WORLD ABOUT US

20 APHRODISIAC FOODS

1. ALLIGATOR.
2. APRICOTS.
3. BEAR'S PAWS.
4. CELERY.
5. CUTTLEFISH (fried).
6. DUCK BEAK.
7. FROG'S LEGS.
8. FRUIT BAT (curried).
9. GARLIC.
10. GINGER.
11. MACARONI.
12. OYSTERS.
13. PARSNIPS (young).
14. PIG'S TROTTERS.
15. PRUNES.
16. RATTLESNAKE.
17. SNAILS.
18. SPINACH.
19. TERMITES.
20. TRUFFLES.

In the unlikely event of being able to lay our hands on bear's paws or rattlesnake at the local supermarket, most of us peak at oysters. They contain dopamine, a chemical said to stimulate desire. Dopamine is also found in broad beans but somehow a dish of broad beans isn't quite as romantic. The tomato was once considered such an aphrodisiac that the Puritans declared it to be poisonous. It became known as the 'love apple' because the English thought the French called it *pomme d'amour.* In fact, they had misheard and it was really known as *pomme du Moor*, having come to France from South America via North Africa. When the mistake was discovered, the tomato's reputation lay in shreds.

> THE WORLD ABOUT US

10 FOODS WHICH ORIGINATE FROM SOUTH AMERICA

1. BUTTER BEAN.

2. GOURD.

3. PEPPER.

4. PINEAPPLE.

5. POTATO.

6. PUMPKIN.

7. RUNNER BEAN.

8. STRAWBERRY.

9. SWEET CORN.

10. TOMATO.

THE WORLD ABOUT US

10 FOODS WHICH ORIGINATE FROM ASIA

1. APRICOT.
2. BANANA.
3. CUCUMBER.
4. EGGPLANT.
5. LEMON.
6. LIME.
7. ONION.
8. ORANGE.
9. PEACH.
10. TANGERINE.

> THE WORLD ABOUT US

10 DISTINCTIVE BRAS

1. The Loving Cup bra of 1979 featured a tiny electronic circuit which signalled when it was safe for sex. Its lights flashed red or green indicating whether sex could result in pregnancy.

2. During the 1970s, cherry-flavoured edible bras were introduced as a tasty tit-bit. Men could also get their teeth into a liquorice-flavoured bra.

3. In 1992, a Somerset man invented a water-filled double-D cup bra. He said that the wearer should add wallpaper paste for an even firmer frontage.

4. From Paris in the 1980s came the Joli'bust, a self-adhesive bra consisting of nothing more than two shaped pieces of sticky plastic fixed beneath the breasts to show off the curves.

5. A new bra on the market is made of hologrammatic fibres, the surface of which creates a 3D impression to make the breasts appear a better shape.

6. Designer André Van Pier created a bra adorned with 3,250 diamonds. It cost £641,000.

7. Scented bras are on the way. The bra of the future will contain micro-pockets of fragrance which will be gradually released throughout the day.

8. There are also plans to introduce a mirrored bra and one impregnated with insect repellent to keep mosquitoes at bay.

9. Another bra of the future is the Smart Bra, featuring nickel-titanium alloys which, according to manufacturers, would 'remember the exact shape of the individual woman's breast'. The technique for using these 'shape-changing' alloys is so sensitive that it has only recently been declassified by the American military.

10. Madonna's famous 'Bullet Bra', worn during her Blonde Ambition tour of 1990, was based on an antique breastplate worn by Italian soldiers.

> THE WORLD ABOUT US

RAINING SPRATS AND FROGS
10 CASES OF ODD WEATHER

1. In October 1947, marine biologist Alan Bajikov observed a downpour of fish while breakfasting with his wife at MARKSVILLE, LOUISIANA. Sunfish, minnows and black bass plummeted from the sky during a gentle shower. No whirlwinds were reported which could have swept the fish up from the nearest stretch of water, the Gulf of Mexico, over 80 miles away. Another fish storm took place at ABERDARE, MID-GLAMORGAN, on February 9, 1859, bringing minnow and smooth-tailed stickleback to earth.

2. Following several weeks of drought, a fierce storm broke one afternoon in August 1814 over FREMONTIERS, near Amiens in France. In the rain which accompanied the storm were dozens of tiny frogs which proceeded to hop around on the ground. Live frogs also fell on LEICESTER, MASSACHUSETTS, on September 7, 1953, landing in gutters and on roofs — proof that they hadn't merely escaped from an overflowing pond.

3. On May 11, 1894, at the height of a hailstorm, a gopher turtle encased in ice fell on BOVINA, eight miles east of Vicksburg, Mississippi. During the same storm, a small block of alabaster, also encased in ice, landed on Vicksburg itself.

4. A deluge of dead birds tumbled from a clear sky on to the streets of BATON ROUGE, LOUISIANA, in November 1896. The only plausible explanation was that the birds, which included wild ducks, catbirds and woodpeckers, had been driven inland by a storm on the Florida coast and had been killed by a sudden temperature change over Baton Rouge.

THE WORLD ABOUT US

5. Lumps of meat fell from a cloudless sky over a 100- by 50-yard area of BATH COUNTY, KENTUCKY, on March 3, 1876. When examined, the meat proved to be lung and muscle tissue, either from a child or a horse. It was thought that the meat may have been disgorged by buzzards but none had been seen in the area, and anyway it would have needed a vast number of birds to produce such a quantity of meat.

6. A 2ft-long alligator fell from the sky at EVANSVILLE, INDIANA, on May 21, 1911, landing on the front doorstep of the home of Mrs. Hiram Winchell. When the creature tried to crawl indoors, it was clubbed to death by Mrs. Winchell and neighbours armed with bed slats.

7. On October 26, 1956, the dead body of a small monkey was found in the back garden of a house in BROADMOOR, CALIFORNIA, by Mrs. Faye Swanson. The post holding her clothes-line had been damaged, presumably by the falling monkey. The only possible explanation for the incident was that the monkey had fallen from an aircraft, yet the local airport insisted that no planes had been carrying such a cargo that night.

8. A rainfall of thousands of living snakes up to 18ins long reportedly fell over the southern half of MEMPHIS, TENNESSEE, in 1877.

9. A crop of peaches — hard, green and the size of golfballs — dropped on a building-site at SHREVEPORT, LOUISIANA, on July 12, 1961. The workmen confirmed that the fruit was coming from the sky and not being thrown. Weathermen said that conditions that day were not conducive to the peaches having been lifted by strong winds.

10. A fall of maggots accompanied a heavy storm at ACAPULCO, MEXICO, on October 5, 1968. Craft assembled for the Olympic yachting events were covered in one-inch long maggots.

THE WORLD ABOUT US

10 REPORTED MONSTERS

1. THE BEAST OF LE GEVAUDAN. Between 1764 and 1767, the village of Saint Etienne de Lugdares, in the mountainous region of France known as Le Gevaudan was terrorised by a ferocious creature which went around killing and mutilating local children. A witness described it as walking on two legs like a man, but having short red hair and a pig-like snout. It was about the size of a donkey. Even the arrival of royal troops failed to quell the beast's appetite until a local nobleman shot it dead with a gun loaded with silver bullets. Some said it was a very large wolf; others insisted that it was a werewolf.

2. THE BEAST OF TRURO. A distant relative of our own Surrey Puma and Beast of Bodmin, the Beast of Truro lurked around the Cape Cod area of Massachusetts in the early 1980s. As pet cats were found slaughtered, speculation grew as to whether the beast was a mountain lion even though none exist in the region. Its identity remains a mystery.

3. CHINESE WILDMAN. Over the years there have been frequent reports of a hairy ape-like creature from Hubei Province in central China. The most convincing sighting was reported in 1940 by Wang Zelin. Travelling along a road in the Shennongija region he heard gunshots in the distance and found a crowd surrounding the corpse of a wild woman. He described the body as being covered in a coat of thick grey/red hair. The face had deep-set eyes and protruding lips.

4. THE FLATHEAD LAKE MONSTER. Visitors to Flathead Lake, Montana, have sometimes spotted something 'huge and black' in the water. A major sighting was in 1963 by Ronald Nixon who calculated the creature to be around 25ft long. Divers scoured the lake in vain and a reward offered for the first good photograph of the monster went unclaimed.

5. GOATMAN. Described as having the upper body of a human, the legs of a goat and cloven hooves, Goatman has been known to leap out on unsuspecting courting couples parked in lovers' lanes in Prince George's County, Virginia. One theory is that the creature was a scientist experimenting on goats at a nearby research station when things went wrong.

THE WORLD ABOUT US

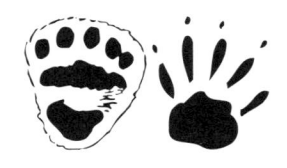

6. THE JERSEY DEVIL. The story goes that somewhere in the wooded Pine Barrens area of New Jersey lurks a monster with a large horse-like head, wings and a long serpent's body. In January 1909, thousands of people claimed to see the Devil or its footprints. Then in 1951 strange screams were apparently heard coming from the woods — the cry of the Jersey Devil.

7. THE LAKE WORTH MONSTER. The sighting in 1969 of a 7ft-tall biped covered in short white fur and with a white goat-like beard sparked a massive monster hunt around Lake Worth, near Fort Worth in Texas. The monster was never found but one tall teenager, wearing white overalls, was shot in the shoulder by an over-zealous hunter.

8. MO-MO. In the summer of 1971 two girls had stopped for a picnic near the town of Louisiana, Missouri, when a half-ape, half-human emerged from some bushes and tried to break into their car. Monster hunts in the area failed to reveal the culprit.

9. MOTHMAN. A weird figure with large wings folded against its back and luminous red eyes appeared to two young couples in 1966 at a roadside outside Point Pleasant, West Virginia. As they drove away in fear, it flew off after them. Other sightings were reported in the area, describing how the creature rose into the air 'like a helicopter'. One caller to the police department in nearby Clarkton insisted that Batman was standing on the roof of the house next door. The following year a bridge over the Ohio River collapsed killing nearly 50 people. The locals blamed Mothman, citing him as an omen of doom. Following the disaster, Mothman seemed to disappear as suddenly as he had arrived.

10. SPRING-HEELED JACK. In 1838, a seemingly respectable man walked into a London police station and recounted how his daughter had been savaged by a cloaked figure which had metallic claws and blue and white flames shooting from his mouth. Renowned for his ability to leap remarkable heights, often by way of escape, Spring-Heeled Jack continued to fascinate and terrify Victorian London. There was even a stage play in his honour in 1863. Who or what he was will almost certainly never be known.

> THE WORLD ABOUT US

10 FORGOTTEN SUPERHEROES

1. BIFF BANNON. A U.S. Marine, big, dumb and strong, who appeared in *Speed Comics* in 1939.

2. BOMBER BURNS. American stunt flier Jack 'Bomber' Burns was attached to the RAF during the Second World War. Shot down by the Germans, he hid in the Scottish Highlands and customised his plane with machine guns, a cannon and a flame-thrower. Featured in *Victory Comics* 1941.

3. ADMIRAL FUDGE. This young, bespectacled adventurer dressed as Napoleon in a comic strip in the *New York World* newspaper, 1908.

4. DR. GRAVES. A pipe-smoking supernaturalist who travelled the world investigating strange phenomena. Appeared in *Charlton Comics*, 1966.

5. HAIRBREADTH HARRY. Teenager Harry (real name Harold Hollingsworth) fought crime in the shape of the moustachioed Rudolph Rassendale. Harry's girlfriend was Belinda Blinks. Appeared as a comic strip in *The Philadelphia Press* in 1906, graduating to six silent films in the 1920s.

6. LANCE O'CASEY. A swashbuckling sailor accompanied everywhere by his first mate, a monkey named Mister Hogan. Featured in *Whizz Comics*, 1940.

7. LARIAT SAM. Violence-hating cowboy with a talking horse, Tippytoes. His sworn enemy was Badlands Meeney. Sam's voice came courtesy of Dayton Allen. Appeared on *The Captain Kangaroo Show* on U.S. TV from 1962.

8. DR. THIRTEEN. Ghost-buster Dr. Terrence Thirteen, a non-believer in the supernatural, made his debut in *DC Comics* in 1951.

9. AGENT KEN THURSTON. A government agent with the code name X, he fought Communists, spies and assorted enemies of the state in *The Man Called X*, a U.S. radio show from 1952 and on TV, 1956-58.

10. TIM TYLER. Orphan Tim and his buddy Spud Slavins set off for Africa in search of adventure and joined a police force known as the Ivory Patrol. A U.S. comic strip from 1928.

> **SPORT**

10 DISCONTINUED OLYMPIC SPORTS

1. CRICKET (1900).
2. CROQUET (1900).
3. GOLF (1900, 1904).
4. JEU DE PAUME (1908).
5. LACROSSE (1904, 1908).
6. MOTORBOATING (1908).
7. POLO (1900, 1908, 1920, 1924, 1936).
8. RACKETS (1908).
9. ROQUE (1904).
10. RUGBY UNION (1900, 1908, 1920, 1924)

These sports were usually included because they were of interest to the host country. So croquet made its solitary appearance in the 1900 Games in Paris. All of the competitors were French, thus giving the host nation a fighting chance of winning gold. Similarly when roque, a form of croquet which was popular in the United States, featured in the 1904 Olympics at St. Louis, all of the players were American. The other obscure sport, *jeu de paume*, is a French variation of tennis, invariably played with the hand. For the one and only Olympic cricket contest, Britain was represented by Devon Wanderers CC who beat a French team composed principally of expatriate Britons in a five-a-side match. And how many people realize that the United States are the reigning Olympic rugby union champions after beating France in 1924…?

SPORT

10 OLYMPIC DEMONSTRATION SPORTS

1. BICYCLE POLO (1908).
2. KORFBALL (1920).
3. AMERICAN FOOTBALL (1932).
4. DOG SLED RACING (1932).
5. GLIDING (1936).
6. BANDY (1952).
7. AUSTRALIAN RULES FOOTBALL (1956).
8. BUDO (1964).
9. WATER SKIING (1972).
10. ROLLER HOCKEY (1992).

As the name implies, demonstration sports were Olympic exhibition events for which no medals were awarded. The 1952 Helsinki Olympics featured a demonstration of bandy, which is like field hockey but played on an ice-covered soccer pitch. A popular sport in neighbouring Sweden, it came as little surprise when the Swedes triumphed. A demonstration of Australian Rules Football at Melbourne in 1956 produced an entertaining 250–135 result while Émile St. Goddard of Canada emerged victorious in the 1932 dog sled racing. But the most bizarre Olympic demonstration sport was surely bicycle polo, back in 1908, even though the Irish won't hear a word against it — for they defeated the might of Germany 3–1.

SPORT

20 SPORTING FAILURES

1. WALLACE WILLIAMS (Virgin Islands) ran in the 1979 Pan-American Games marathon, but was so slow that by the time he reached the stadium it was locked and everyone had gone home.

2. Boxer RALPH WALTON of the United States was still adjusting his gumshield when he was knocked out by Al Couture just half a second into their 1946 bout at Lewiston, Maine.

3. ROBERTO ALVAREZ (Mexico) finished so far behind in the 50-kilometre cross-country skiing at the 1988 Winter Olympics that worried officials sent out a search party to look for him.

4. Playing the 130-yard 16th hole at the 1912 Shawnee Invitational for Ladies, American golfer MAUD McINNES saw her drive land in the Binniekill River and float downstream. Undeterred, she clambered into a boat and, with her husband at the oars, set off in pursuit of her ball. Eventually, a mile and a half further down the river, after a number of unsuccessful attempts, she managed to hit the ball on to dry land. She then had to play back through a wood to reach the 16th green. Two hours after her tee shot, she holed out for a 166 — 163 over par for the hole.

5. Film star TREVOR HOWARD was an ardent cricketer. One day in 1960 he got up at 5am to drive 180 miles to Buxton, Derbyshire, for a match only to be out first ball.

6. To combat the heat in the 1950 Tour de France, ABD-EL KADER ZAAG drank a bottle of wine offered by a spectator and promptly fell off his bike. After sleeping it off by the roadside, he climbed back in the saddle and sped off...in the wrong direction.

7. ANTONIN MILORDIS (Greece) fell 18 times during his slalom ski run at the 1952 Winter Olympics. His time for one run was longer than the winner's two-run total.

8. In May 1986, 52-year-old PEDRO GATICA cycled from his home in Agentina to Mexico for the soccer World Cup, only to find on arrival that he couldn't afford to get in. While he haggled for a ticket, thieves stole his bike.

9. Cuban postman FELIZ CARVAJAL was denied a medal in the 1904 Olympic marathon when he stopped en route to talk to spectators and eat unripe fruit. The resulting indigestion relegated him to fourth place.

10. Russian athlete IVANON VYACHESLAV was so thrilled to win a medal at the 1956 Melbourne Olympics that he hurled it high into the air in jubilation. Unfortunately it came down in Lake Wendouree where, despite a frantic search, it remains to this day.

SPORT

11. Goalkeeper ISADORE IRANDIR of Brazilian team Rio Preto was on his knees in the goalmouth saying his traditional pre-match prayers as opponents Corinthians kicked off. Three seconds later, he was just concluding his beseechments to the Almighty when a 60-yard shot from Roberto Rivelino flew past his ear into the net.

12. Batting at Kalgoorlie, Australia, in the 1970s cricketer STAN DAWSON was hit by a delivery which ignited a box of matches in his pocket. As he tried to beat down the flames, he was run out.

13. Waving to crowds after finishing fourth in the 500cc US Motor Cycle Grand Prix at Laguna Seca, in 1989, Australia's KEVIN MAGEE fell off on his lap of honour and broke a leg.

14. Driving off at the 17th tee at Lyme Regis, Dorset, 69-year-old DEREK GATLEY was half-way through his backswing when the steel shaft snapped and the club struck him on the back of the head, knocking him out. When he came to, a rueful Mr. Gatley admitted: 'It was the first thing I'd hit all day!'

15. At the 1929 American Football Rosebowl, California centre ROY RIEGELS ran nearly half the length of the field with the ball — but in the wrong direction, towards his own goal. 'Wrong-Way Riegels' became an overnight celebrity, receiving an offer of marriage in which he and his bride would walk up the aisle instead of down!

16. Preparing for a bout at the 1992 New York Golden Gloves Championships, boxer DANIEL CARUSO psyched himself up by pounding his gloves into his face. In doing so, he broke his nose and was declared unfit to box.

17. After travelling all the way from New York to Sandwich, Kent, for the 1937 Amateur Golf Championship, BRIGADIER-GENERAL CRITCHLEY arrived six minutes late and was disqualified.

18. Reigning Tour de France champion PEDRO DELGADO of Spain only finished third in 1989 after losing three minutes at the start signing autographs.

19. Referee HENNING ERIKSTRUP was about to blow the final whistle at a 1960 Danish League match between Norager and Ebeltoft when his dentures fell out. As he scrambled around on the pitch trying to recover them, Ebeltoft equalised. However Mr. Erikstrup disallowed the goal, replaced his teeth and blew for full-time.

20. After beating 1,000 rivals in a gruelling 500-mile race, PERCY the racing pigeon flopped down exhausted in his Sheffield loft...and was promptly eaten by the neighbourhood cat.

> SPORT

10 BIZARRE SPORTING EVENTS

1. An ingenious alternative to England's famous Henley-on-Thames Regatta is staged each October at Alice Springs in Australia's Northern Territory. It is the **HENLEY-ON-TODD REGATTA**, the difference between the Thames and the Todd being that the Todd River is invariably dry. The competing canoes are bottomless, the crews' legs protruding through the holes so that the teams run along the river bed.

2. Back in the 19th century, Yorkshire folk bound for Blackpool would stop off at the Corner Pin public house at Ramsbottom near Manchester. One day they started throwing stones at the Yorkshire puddings which had been left to cool down on the ledges of the pub roof prior to lunch. Seeing this, the landlord decided to instigate a War of the Roses with Lancashire black puddings replacing stones. Thus since 1837, competitors have hurled black puddings on to the roof of the Corner Pin in a bid to dislodge the Yorkshire puddings nestling there. The contests has acquired the title of the **WORLD BLACK PUDDING KNOCKING CHAMPIONSHIPS** and attracts entrants from as far afield as the United States, Australia, Canada and Germany. Each competitor is permitted three lobs, a ladder being used to replace the fallen Yorkshire puddings. The first prize is the winner's height in beer.

3. Tobacco-spitting is the name of the game at the annual **CALICO TOBACCO CHEWING AND SPITTING CHAMPIONSHIPS** near Barstow, California. Wads have been known to be ejected distances of over 47 feet.

4. The sport of brick-throwing is recognized by an international contest held each July at **STROUD, NEW SOUTH WALES**, between teams representing the Australian, English, American and Canadian towns named Stroud. So that the ladies don't feel left out, there is also a rolling-pin-throwing contest.

5. The **WORLD FLOUNDER-TRAMPING CHAMPIONSHIPS** were first staged in 1976 to settle a wager as to who could catch the biggest flounder in

> **SPORT**

Scotland's Urr estuary. The flounder, a flat-fish, lies on the bottom of the shallow estuary and buries itself in the mud when the tide goes out. Some 200 competitors wade chest-high into the water with bare feet, searching for the tell-tale wriggle of the flounder beneath their toes. The fish can then be captured either with a three-pronged spear called a leister or by manual dexterity. The flounder must be alive at the weigh-in.

6. The BEER CAN REGATTA is raced each June off Mindil Beach at Darwin in Australia's Northern Territory. All of the craft are assembled from beer and soft drinks cans, the result being anything from a simple raft to an intricate galleon.

7. Bed-pushers from all over Britain converge on North Yorkshire each year for the KNARESBOROUGH BED RACE. The main obstacle on the gruelling two-mile course is the River Nidd.

8. The inaugural WORLD WORM-CHARMING CHAMPIONSHIPS took place at Willaston, Cheshire, in 1980. The winner charmed 511 worms out of his three-metre-square plot in the allotted half-hour. The worms are coaxed to the surface by vibrating garden forks and other implements in the soil. Water may also be employed but competitors must drink a sample before use. This rule follows a spate of unsavoury incidents where the water was laced with washing-up liquid, a banned stimulant which irritates the worm's skin and drives it illegally to the surface.

9. The highlight of the VANCOUVER SEA FESTIVAL each July is the Nanaimo to Vancouver bathtub race across the choppy waters of the Strait of Georgia.

10. Llanwrtyd Wells in Powys, Wales, is the venue for the annual WORLD BOG-SNORKELLING CHAMPIONSHIPS. Entrants must swim 60 yards with their snorkels through a murky, weed-infested peat bog in as fast a time as possible. There is rarely any great rush to hug the winner....

> SPORT

20 SPORTS STARS WHO HAVE APPEARED IN FILMS

1. **MUHAMMAD ALI.** The world heavyweight boxing champion played himself in *The Greatest* (1977) and *Body and Soul* (1981). He also appeared as a young fighter in Requiem for a Heavyweight (1962) and as Gideon Jackson, the first black U.S. Senator, in the 1979 TV movie *Freedom Road*.

2. **VIJAY AMRITRAJ.** The Indian tennis player appeared as himself in the 1983 James Bond movie *Octopussy*.

3. **MARIO ANDRETTI.** The American racing driver who became world champion in 1978 played himself in a film of that year, *Speed Fever*. Austrian ace **NIKKI LAUDA** appeared in the same picture.

4. **DANNY BLANCHFLOWER.** The former Tottenham and Northern Ireland soccer international portrayed himself in the 1983 movie *Those Glory Glory Days*.

5. **BJORN BORG.** The Swedish tennis champion appeared as himself in the 1979 production *Racquet*.

6. **JACK BRABHAM.** The Australian three-times world motor racing champion played himself in the 1961 production *The Green Helmet*.

7. **HENRY COOPER.** In 1975, the former British heavyweight boxing champion starred as prizefighter John Gully in *Royal Flash*.

8. **BUSTER CRABBE.** The 1932 Olympic 400-metre freestyle swimming champion made his film debut the following year as Karpa the Lion Man in *King of the Jungle*. He went on to appear in a further 52 movies, most notably as *Flash Gordon* and *Buck Rogers*.

9. **STEVE DONAGHUE.** The American jockey played Steve Baxter, hero of four

SPORT

1926 films about horse-racing, *Riding for a King*, *Beating the Book*, *The Golden Spurs* and *The Stolen Favourite*.

10. **BRUCE JENNER.** The American decathlete who won gold at the 1976 Olympics played an uptight lawyer in the 1980 flop *Can't Stop the Music.*

11. **JEAN-CLAUDE KILLY.** The French skiing ace appeared as a devious ski instructor in the 1972 movie *Snow Job.*

12. **JIM LAKER.** The English off-spinner appeared with team-mates **DENIS COMPTON, LEN HUTTON** and **ALEC BEDSER** in the 1953 cricketing epic *The Final Test*. They all played themselves.

13. **SUZANNE LENGLEN.** The French tennis champion appeared as herself in the 1935 film *Things Are Looking Up.*

14. **JOE LOUIS.** The newly-crowned world heavyweight boxing champion played a hungry young fighter in the all-black Spirit of Youth in 1938. .

15. **STIRLING MOSS.** The charismatic British motor-racing driver appeared alongside **DAVID NIVEN** in the 1967 film *Casino Royale.*

16. **ILIE NASTASE.** The Romanian tennis champion appeared as himself in the 1979 movie *Players.*

17. **PELÉ.** The Brazilian soccer star played the footballing hero in *Hotshot* (1987).

18. **DENNIS RODMAN.** The colourful Chicago Bulls basketball star appeared in the 1997 film *Double Team.*

19. **BARRY SHEENE.** The world motorcycling champion played himself in the 1983 film *Space Riders.*

20. **BOMBARDIER BILLY WELLS.** The British heavyweight boxing champion starred as the pilot in the 1919 film *The Silver Lining* and played the hangman in the 1952 film *The Beggar's Opera* which starred Laurence Olivier.

SPORT

10 SPORTS STARS WHO HAVE BEEN THE SUBJECT OF FILMS

1. **HAROLD ABRAHAMS.** The 1924 Olympic 100 metres champion was played by Ben Cross in the 1981 hit *Chariots of Fire*.

2. **NADIA COMANECI.** The tiny Romanian gymnast, star of the 1976 Montreal Olympics, was played by Leslie Weiner (as a youngster) and Johann Carlo (in adulthood) in the 1984 movie *Nadia*.

3. **DAWN FRASER.** The Australian triple gold-medallist swimmer, later banned for stealing a flag at the Tokyo Olympics, was portrayed by Bronwyn Mackay-Payne in the 1979 movie *Dawn*.

4. **BEN HOGAN.** Glenn Ford played the U.S. golfer in the film *Follow the Sun*.

5. **ANNETTE KELLERMAN.** Esther Williams starred as Australian swimmer Annette Kellerman in the 1952 movie *Million Dollar Mermaid*.

6. **BOB MATHIAS.** The double Olympic decathlon-winner (1948 and 1952) played himself in the 1954 movie *The Bob Mathias Story*.

7. **KNUTE ROCKNE.** The celebrated Football coach was played by Pat O'Brien in the 1940 biopic *Knute Rockne, All American*. Ronald Reagan co-starred.

8. **WILMA RUDOLPH.** Shirley Jo Finney played the brilliant American Olympic sprinter in the 1977 TV movie *Wilma*.

9. **JOHN L. SULLIVAN.** The 'Boston Strong Boy', heavyweight boxing champion from 1882 to 1892, was played by Greg McClure in *The Great John L*.

10. **JIM THORPE.** Was played by Burt Lancaster in the 1951 film *All-American*.

> SPORT

10 SURPRISING SPORTSMEN

1. **MATTHEW ARNOLD.** The poet was an accomplished high-jumper and once vaulted a set of 5ft 3in high spiked railings at Oxford for a bet.

2. **ARNOLD BENNETT.** The author was no mean footballer and played for his school's First Eleven.

3. **SIR ARTHUR CONAN DOYLE.** The creator of Sherlock Holmes played soccer for Portsmouth and cricket for the M.C.C. He hit a century on his debut, had bowling figures of 7-51 against Cambridgeshire and once bowled out the great W.G. Grace.

4. **BILLY JOEL.** The American singer was a welterweight boxing champion in his youth.

5. **HUGH LAURIE.** The comedian rowed for the defeated Cambridge crew in the 1980 University Boat Race.

6. **JOHNNY MATHIS.** In 1955, the singer was ranked joint 85th in the world for the high jump.

7. **LIAM NEESON.** The Irish actor was a keen boxer in his younger days.

8. **RYAN O'NEAL.** The Hollywood star boxed as a teenager in Golden Gloves contests.

9. **EDGAR ALLAN POE.** The American author was an accomplished exponent of the long jump.

10. **JAMES WHALE.** Broadcaster Whale is a former Surrey Junior Archery Champion.

> SPORT

10 SUPERSTITIOUS SPORTSMEN

1. JACK BERRY. The English racehorse trainer is never seen in public without his trademark red shirt. The superstition began in his early twenties when Berry was an aspiring jockey. He bought a red shirt prior to a meeting at Ayr and the next day he wore the shirt and rode a winner. After that, whenever he rode a fancied horse, he put on the red shirt to bring him luck. He now has a vast collection, sent to him by well-wishers and owners who would be most aggrieved if he was wearing anything but a red shirt on race day.

2. BJORN BORG. The Swedish tennis maestro always stopped shaving four days before a major championship. Then before each match he would pack his bag so that all ten racquets were arranged in descending order of tension. The tension testing would take up to an hour. When travelling to Wimbledon, he was always driven over Hammersmith Bridge, never Putney Bridge — and the car had to possess a radio. His parents were equally superstitious. Every year, they alternated between watching their son at Wimbledon and at the French Open in Paris, convinced that to attend both championships in the same year would bring his run of success to an end. Borg's mother, Margarethe, always made a point of sucking a sweet during the final set. At Wimbledon in 1979, after Borg had reached three match points, opponent Roscoe Tanner rallied to deuce. Mrs. Borg decided to spit the sweet on the floor but quickly realized the folly of her actions, picked it up and slipped it back in her mouth. For mother and son there was soon the delicious taste of another victory.

3. STEVE CLARIDGE. The much-travelled footballer has a curious pre-match ritual when the team stays in a hotel. He always has to have a room on his own and the first thing he does is to remove the hotel sheets from the bed and replace them with ones he has brought from home. His favourite pre-match meal is Rice Krispies and baked beans — sometimes together.

4. PHIL GRIDELET. Footballer Phil Gridelet always insists on being the last player to come out onto the pitch at the start of each half. Usually this presents no problem but when his team, Southend United, met Ipswich in February 1997 his superstition was really put to the test — for team-mate Andy Rammell was having problems with his contact lenses at half-time

SPORT

and was late out for the second half. Instead of bolstering the numbers, Gridelet steadfastly stayed with him in the dressing-room, forcing Southend to kick off with just nine players. Manager Ronnie Whelan labelled Gridelet's decision 'crazy'.

5. ALBERT KNIGHT. The Leicestershire cricketer who played for England in 1903 was a lay preacher and before each innings would go down on his knees at the crease to pray for help from above. Playing at Middlesex, his antics brought a new meaning to the Lord's Prayer.

6. JACK NICKLAUS. The great American golfer always carries three pennies in his pocket at tournaments and, when he marks the ball, always does it with the tails side up.

7. GARY PLAYER. When the little South African opens a brand-new box of golf balls, he immediately discards all the odd-numbered balls and plays only with the even-numbered ones.

8. GRAHAM THORNER. Former jump jockey Graham Thorner hated using anything new. He would always get someone else to break in a new saddle or a new pair of breeches for him, and rather than wear a new set of colours he would often jump up and down on them first, just to create that 'used' look. He also insisted on wearing the same lucky underpants and would never ride with a green saddle-pad until he rode a winner with one at Newton Abbot and thereafter demanded a green saddle-pad for every race.

9. JACK TINN. The diminutive Geordie who guided Portsmouth Football Club to three FA Cup finals attributed his success to his lucky spats. Throughout the 1939 Cup run, which ended in a 4-1 victory over Wolves at Wembley, Tinn wore the magical spats, which were religiously put on for him by the same player before every match.

10. LEV YASHIN. The former Russian international goalkeeper always took two caps to a match. He wore one and put the other behind him in the net for luck.

SPORT

10 FOOTBALLERS' NICKNAMES

1. **THE BLACK PANTHER** (Eusebio).

2. **BUDGIE** (Johnny Byrne).

3. **THE CAT** (Peter Bonetti).

4. **CRAZY HORSE** (Emlyn Hughes).

5. **THE FLYING PIG** (Tommy Lawrence).

6. **THE GIRAFFE** (Jack Charlton).

7. **LITTLE BIRD** (Garrincha).

8. **SNIFFER** (Allan Clarke).

9. **SPARKY** (Mark Hughes).

10. **THE VULTURE** (Emilio Butragueno).

> **SPORT**

10 BOXERS' NICKNAMES

1. THE AMBLING ALP (Primo Carnera).

2. THE BROCKTON BLOCKBUSTER (Rocky Marciano).

3. THE BROWN BOMBER (Joe Louis).

4. THE FIGHTING MARINE (Gene Tunney).

5. GENTLEMAN JIM (James J. Corbett).

6. THE LIVERMORE LARRUPER (Max Baer).

7. THE LOUISVILLE LIP (Muhammad Ali).

8. THE MANASSA MAULER (Jack Dempsey).

9. THE MICHIGAN ASSASSIN (Stanley Ketchel).

10. ORCHID MAN (Georges Carpentier).

10 FATHER AND SON GOLFERS

1. When BUDDY ALEXANDER won the 1986 U.S. Amateur Championship, he was not the first in the family to taste golfing success. His father SKIP won two PGA events back in 1948 and played for the United States Ryder Cup team in 1949 and 1951.

2. PERCY ALLISS and his son PETER both played for Britain in the Ryder Cup, the former three times and the latter eight.

3. The final of the 1952 Swiss Amateur Championship was contested by father and son ANTOINE and ANDRÉ BARRAS. The son won.

4. JOE CARR and his sons RODDY and JOHN have all represented Ireland at golf.

5. CLAYTON HEAFNER was a member of the American Ryder Cup teams of 1949 and 1951 and his son VANCE played for the 1977 American Walker Cup team.

6. American Ryder Cup player DAVIS LOVE III is, unsurprisingly, the son of DAVIS LOVE II who finished equal sixth in the 1969 British Open.

7. OLD TOM MORRIS (1861, 1862, 1864, 1867) and YOUNG TOM MORRIS (1868, 1869, 1870, 1872) both won the British Open. Young Tom's triumph in 1868 meant that he succeeded his father as champion, the only time this has ever happened in a major tournament.

8. WILLIE PARK SR. (1860, 1863, 1866, 1875) and WILLIE PARK JR. (1889) also both won the British Open.

9. GARY PLAYER's son WAYNE played for South Africa in the 1980 World Amateur Team Championship.

10. HARRY VARDON, six times winner of the British Open, had a younger brother TOM who finished runner-up to him in the 1903 championship at Prestwick.

SPORT

10 BROTHERLY GOLFERS

1. When MIGUEL BALLESTEROS won the 1983 Timex Open in Biarritz, he was beginning to emerge from the shadows of illustrious brother SEVERIANO who had already won the U.S. Masters and British Open.

2. Brothers JAY and LIONEL HEBERT both played for the United States in the Ryder Cup — Lionel in 1957, Jay in 1959 and 1961. They have also both won the U.S. PGA Championship — Lionel in 1957 and Jay in 1960.

3. HAROLD and ALAN HENNING are both former winners of the South African Open.

4. In 1963, brothers BERNARD and GEOFFREY HUNT represented Great Britain and Ireland in the Ryder Cup in Atlanta.

5. ANGEL and SEBASTIAN MIGUEL both won the Spanish Open in the early 1960s.

6. In 1910, ALEX SMITH defeated his brother, MACDONALD, in a play-off for the U.S. Open. Another brother, WILLIE, had won the title in 1899. And in 1906, Alex had finished first with Willie as runner-up.

7. In 1954, PETER TOOGOOD won the Australian Amateur Championship just ahead of brother JOHN. Two years later, they finished first and third in the Tasmanian Open. Sandwiched between them in second place was their father ALFRED.

8. After JOE TURNESA had finished second in the U.S. PGA Championship of 1927, brother JIM went one better, winning the title in 1952. A third brother, WILLIE, twice won the U.S. Amateur Championship.

9. America's LANNY WADKINS was U.S. PGA champion in 1977 and the following year younger brother BOBBY won the inaugural European Open.

10. CHARLES, ERNEST and REG WHITCOMBE all played for Britain in the Ryder Cup, Charles and Ernest being paired together in the 1935 foursomes.

SPORT

THE WORLD'S FIRST 10 GOLF CLUBS

1. HONOURABLE COMPANY OF EDINBURGH GOLFERS	1744.
2. GOLF CLUB OF ST. ANDREWS (later the Royal And Ancient)	1754.
3. BRUNTSFIELD LINKS GOLFING SOCIETY	1761.
4. ROYAL BLACKHEATH	1766.
5. ROYAL MUSSELBURGH	1774.
6. ROYAL ABERDEEN	1780.
7. GLASGOW	1787.
8. DUNBAR	1794.
9. BURNTISLAND	1797.
10. ROYAL ALBERT, MONTROSE	1810.

SPORT

THE FIRST 20 COUNTRIES TO TAKE UP GOLF

(BASED ON THE DATE OF THE OLDEST CLUB TO HAVE ENJOYED CONTINUOUS EXISTENCE)

1. SCOTLAND (1744) — Honourable Company of Edinburgh Golfers.
2. ENGLAND (1766) — Royal Blackheath.
3. INDIA (1829) — Royal Calcutta.
4. FRANCE (1856) — Pau.
5. PAKISTAN (1857) — Lahore Gymkhana.
6. JAMAICA (1868) — Manchester.
7. INDONESIA (1872) — Jakarta.
8. CANADA (1873) — Royal Montreal.
9. SRI LANKA (1879) — Royal Colombo.
10. IRELAND (1881) — Royal Belfast.
11. ITALY (1885) — Roma.   SOUTH AFRICA (1885) — Royal Cape.
13. WALES (1888) — Tenby.   BELGIUM (1888) — Royal Antwerp.
    UNITED STATES (1888) — St. Andrews (Yonkers), New York.
    MALAYSIA (1888) — Perak at Taipang.
17. HONG KONG (1889) — Royal Hong Kong.
    ARGENTINA (1889) — Lomas, Buenos Aires.
19. PORTUGAL (1890) — Oporto.
    THAILAND (1890) — Royal Bangkok.

10 BAD TEMPERED GOLFERS

1. Former British Ryder Cup player BRIAN BARNES 12-putted a hole in the 1968 French Open at St. Cloud after losing his temper. Playing the second round, he had taken three shots to the eighth and was left with a putt of less than a yard. But when he missed it, he began angrily stabbing at the ball while it was still moving, incurring a further penalty for standing astride the line of a putt. He ended up taking 15 before the ball finally dropped into the hole.

2. After his Florida University team had lost to Wake Forest University, young ANDY BEAN took out his frustration on a golf ball by trying to eat it. He sank his teeth into the cover of the ball, bit off a large chunk and handed it to a friend with the words: 'Here, take it. I've eaten my last golf ball. I'm going off the diet.'

3. TOMMY BOLT had a reputation for hurling his clubs around when things went wrong. Nicknamed 'Thunder-Bolt', he threw his driver into a lake at the 1960 U.S. Open at Cherry Hills, Colorado and another time had to pay a deep-sea diver $75 to retrieve the driver from the bottom of a canal. After one particularly volatile round, partner Jimmy Demaret remarked that Bolt's putter had spent 'more time in the air than Lindbergh.'

4. After missing two simple putts at Oakmont Country Club in 1919, American golfer CHICK EVANS was so angry with himself that he holed out with the handle of his umbrella.

5. Frustrated by the slow play of his partners at the 1968 Los Angeles Open, fiery American BOB GOALBY abandoned them half-way round and went off and finished alone. On another occasion he was so disgusted with one shot that he threw himself, fully-clothed, into a water hazard!

SPORT

6. According to Sam Snead, American **CLAYTON HEAFNER** was 'the most even-tempered golfer I ever saw. He was mad all the time.' Heafner once stormed off the first tee because the starter pronounced his name incorrectly, while another starter incurred his wrath by referring to a shot from a tree which Heafner had been forced to play in the corresponding event the previous year. To ensure there was no repetition Heafner marched off the tee, threw his clubs in the car and drove out of the event in a cloud of dust.

7. American golfer **KY LAFFOON**, who played in the 1935 Ryder Cup, had a love-hate relationship with his putter. After one missed putt he was seen trying to strangle the club and, when that failed, he attempted to drown it — not by hurling it into a lake but by actually holding it down under water! Finally he decided to punish it by tying it with string to the bumper of his car and allowing it to bruise itself on the tarmac as he drove to the next tournament. On another occasion, he angrily broke his putter by smashing it against his foot. Unfortunately the impact also broke his toe.

8. **NORMAN VON NIDA**, an Australian post-war professional, exploded in a bunker during a tournament in England. Unable to extricate his ball, he vented his anger on the lump of turf which formed the insurmountable overhang. Hacking away at it with his clubs until he had completely destroyed it, he proceeded to hide the pieces in nearby bushes. When challenged about his behaviour, he insisted that he had been merely been 'tidying up'.

9. Texan golfer **LEFTY STACKHOUSE** punished himself after one poor shot by throwing himself into a thorn hedge. He was also seen to thrash an entire set of clubs into pieces against a tree stump.

10. Putting at Bethesda Congressional Country Club, Maryland, in 1979, 66-year-old physician Dr. **SHERMAN A. THOMAS** was so distracted by the honking of a nearby Canadian goose that he chased the bird and felled it with a blow to the head. Up before the local beak, he was fined $500 for killing a goose out of season.

THE 10 LONGEST WINNING SEQUENCES BY A RACEHORSE

1. CAMARERO (56). From April 1953 to August 1955, won his first 56 races in Puerto Rico. He eventually finished with a career record of 73 wins from 77 races over distances from five to nine furlongs.

2. KINCSEM (54). The Hungarian-bred mare was never beaten, winning ten races as a two-year-old in 1876, 17 at three years, 15 at four years and 12 at five. She raced all over the world at distances of anything from five furlongs to two and a half miles.

3. GALGO JR. (39). Between 1930 and 1931, Galgo Jr. won 39 successive races in Puerto Rico.

4. LEVIATHAN (23). Racing almost exclusively in Virginia, Leviathan chalked up an impressive sequence in long-distance events between 1797 and 1801. He retired with 24 wins from 30 starts.

5. MISS PETTY (22). A sharp sprinter, Miss Petty remained unbeaten in minor Queensland events between 1985 and 1989.

6. POOKER T (22). Competing in modest claiming races in Puerto Rico in 1962, Pooker T notched up 24 wins, 22 of them in succession.

7. BOND'S FIRST CONSUL (21). The champion of the northern states of America, Joshua Bond's horse won the first 21 races of his career from 1801 to 1806.

8. LOTTERY (21). An outstanding American mare, Lottery lost only the first of her 22 races, winning major Jockey Club races at South Carolina in 1808 and 1810.

9. METEOR (21). Although small in stature, British-trained Meteor won 30 of his 33 starts from 1786, mostly at Newmarket.

10. PICNIC IN THE PARK (21). This horse broke the Australasian record of 19 consecutive wins which had stood for over 60 years when trotting up in 21 successive sprint races at lowly Queensland 'bush' tracks between 1984 and 1985.

SPORT

THE FIRST 10 U.S. TRIPLE CROWN WINNERS

(THE TRIPLE CROWN COMPRISES THE KENTUCKY DERBY, THE PREAKNESS STAKES AND THE BELMONT STAKES)

1. **SIR BARTON (1919)** arrived at the Kentucky Derby as a maiden after six starts and with the job of pacemaker for Billy Kelly. Instead Sir Barton won by five lengths, took the Preakness four days later by four lengths and within a month had romped home in the Belmont.

2. **GALLANT FOX (1930)** was a disappointment as a two-year-old but blossomed the following year. Retired after winning 11 of his 17 races.

3. **OMAHA (1935).** A Gallant Fox foal, Omaha completed the treble despite being beaten in the Withers Stakes in the short period between the Preakness and the Belmont.

4. **WAR ADMIRAL (1937)** remained unbeaten as a three-year-old, running up eight victories. Finished with a career record of 21 wins from 26 starts.

5. **WHIRLAWAY (1941)** was named U.S. Horse of the Year at both three and four. Despite a tendency to veer right under pressure, he retired with earnings of $561,161 but proved a flop as a sire.

6. **COUNT FLEET (1943)** was invincible as a three-year-old, culminating in a Belmont victory by 25 lengths. Unfortunately he suffered an injury in that race which forced his retirement.

7. **ASSAULT (1946)** won at 71-1 as a two-year-old but raced at much shorter prices as a successful three-year-old. He was still winning at six and retired the following year with 18 wins from 42 starts.

8. **CITATION (1948)** won nine out of ten as a juvenile and 19 out of 20 at three. Injury curtailed his subsequent appearances but he still won over $1 million.

9. **SECRETARIAT (1973)** set track records for both the Kentucky Derby and the Belmont, a race he won by a record 31 lengths.

10. **SEATTLE SLEW (1977)** fetched only $17,500 as a yearling but retired with 14 wins from 17 starts. He became America's champion sire in 1984.

SPORT

MICHAEL SCHUMACHER'S 10 BEST CRASH EXCUSES

1. 1991 Australian GP with Jean Alesi:
'I got wheel spin over a puddle and went sideways. It didn't seem like a problem, but Alesi tried to pass me and hit my right front wheel.'

2. 1992 French GP with Ayrton Senna:
'I tried to pass, he came in and I just couldn't stop.'

3. 1993 Japanese GP with Damon Hill: 'I was trying to stay close to Gerhard Berger to stop Hill from moving inside, but he did and I hit his wheel.'

4. 1994 Australian GP with Damon Hill: 'I went over grass and hit a wall, then I just wanted to run into the next corner and suddenly saw Damon next to me. We just hit each other.'

5. 1995 British GP with Damon Hill: 'I think what Damon did was totally unnecessary. In fact it was really stupid. There was no room for two cars.'

6. 1995 Italian GP with Damon Hill: 'I felt a big bang and Damon crashed into me. It was not a slight touch — he really crashed into me.'

7. 1995 Australian GP with Jean Alesi:
'I don't understand what was going on in his brain. Was it switched off?'

8. 1997 Luxembourg GP with Ralf Schumacher: 'It's a shame that the incident happened with my brother but I don't think anyone is to blame.'

9. 1997 European GP with Jacques Villeneuve: 'He tried a rather optimistic attack. It worked for him but not for me.'

10. 1998 Argentinian GP with David Coulthard:
'I went for the gap but he seemed to close the door. I did not want to lift off because I felt I had the momentum to get through.'

SPORT

10 DRIVERS WHO NEVER QUALIFIED FOR A FORMULA ONE GRAND PRIX

1. **GIOVANNA AMATA.** Italian woman driver who launched unsuccessful bids to qualify for the 1992 Grands Prix of South Africa, Mexico and Brazil.

2. **GARY BRABHAM.** Son of Sir Jack failed to qualify in 1990.

3. **COLIN CHAPMAN.** The future Lotus supremo failed in his bid to qualify for the 1956 French Grand Prix at Reims driving a Vanwall.

4. **KEVIN COGAN.** The U.S. Indy Car winner made futile attempts at the Grand Prix circuit in 1980 and 1981.

5. **BERNIE ECCLESTONE.** The man who is now the driving force behind Formula One failed to qualify in a Connaught in 1958 at Monaco and Silverstone.

6. **DIVINA GALICA.** British lady skier who unsuccessfully tried her hand at Formula One in 1976 and 1978.

7. **NAOKI HATTORI.** The Japanese motor sport journalist failed to make the starting grid in 1991.

8. **PERRY McCARTHY.** British enthusiast who, driving a Moda in 1992, entered eight Grands Prix without success.

9. **OTTO STUPPACHER.** The Austrian missed his chance at Monza in 1976 when, having failed to qualify in his Tyrrell, he left the circuit. However Hunt, Mass and Watson had their times disallowed, which would have allowed Stuppacher in the race. But by that time he was back in Vienna!

10. **JACQUES VILLENEUVE.** Younger brother of Gilles and uncle of World Champion Jacques, he tried twice in 1981 and once in 1983 without success.

10 GRAND PRIX DRIVERS WHO DIED IN NON-RACING ACCIDENTS

1. **GEORGES BOILLOT** (1916): shot down in a plane by Germans.

2. **ANDRÉ BOILLOT** (1932): killed in a road crash.

3. **WILBUR SHAW** (1954): died in a plane crash.

4. **MIKE HAWTHORN** (1959): died in a car crash on the Guildford by-pass.

5. **GUISEPPE FARINA** (1966): killed in a road accident on his way to the French GP.

6. **GRAHAM HILL** (1975): killed in a plane crash on a golf course near Barnet, Hertfordshire.

7. **CARLOS PACE** (1977): died in a plane crash.

8. **MIKE HAILWOOD** (1981): died in a road crash near Tanworth-in-Arden, Warwickshire.

9. **ELIO DE ANGELIS** (1986): killed while testing at Paul Ricard, Provence.

10. **DIDIER PIRONI** (1987): died in a power-boat accident off the Isle of Wight.

SPORT

10 GRAND PRIX DRIVERS KILLED IN PRACTICE SESSIONS

1. **DAVID BRUCE-BROWN (1912):** United States GP at Milwaukee.

2. **ACHILLE VARZI (1948):** Swiss GP at Berne.

3. **HARRY SCHELL (1960):** killed at Silverstone on Friday May 13.

4. **RICARDO RODRIGUEZ (1962):** Mexican GP.

5. **MIKE SPENCE (1968):** Indianapolis 500.

6. **JOCHEN RINDT (1970):** Italian GP at Monza.

7. **FRANÇOIS CEVERT (1974):** United States GP, Watkins Glen.

8. **PETER REVSON (1974):** Kyalami, South Africa.

9. **PATRICK DEPAILLER (1980):** German GP at Hockenheim.

10. **GILLES VILLENEUVE (1982):** Zolder, Belgium.

> **THE 20TH CENTURY**

10 THINGS WHICH HAPPENED ON JANUARY 1, 1900

1. While the siege of Mafeking continued in the Boer War, the annual conference of the Incorporated Society of Musicians opened in Scarborough.

2. The Michigan–Mississippi canal was opened.

3. A verdict of accidental death was returned on the victims of the Brighton railway collision.

4. Nigeria became a British protectorate.

5. The South Goodwin Lightship was returned to its moorings after drifting in high winds.

6. Arthur Quiller-Couch's latest novel *The Ship of Stars* was published.

7. In honour of the famous explorer, the Livingstone Exhibition was opened at St. Martin's Town Hall, London.

8. Police investigated the death of 75-year-old Nicholas Theodore de Fischer who died after being mugged in Kensington.

9. In the First Division of the Football League, lowly Glossop surprised Newcastle United 3–2. Nevertheless Glossop went on to finish bottom of the table.

10. In Berlin the German emperor delivered a rousing speech to the German army extolling the strength of the German empire.

> THE 20TH CENTURY

10 REASONS FOR NOT WEARING A MOUSTACHE

(AS GIVEN TO THE HAIRDRESSER AND TOILET REQUISITES GAZETTE IN 1909)

1. 'I have a natural repulsion to seeing hair on a man's face.'

2. 'All nice men, actors, clergymen and other professional men are clean-shaven. Men without a moustache look more intelligent.'

3. 'A bad-tempered, cynical or criminal mouth may be hidden by a moustache.'

4. 'I much prefer a clean-shaven man. I do not consider a moustache hygienic.'

5. 'Decidedly give me a clean-shaven man if he has a good mouth and chin. Men with weak chins should be made to wear beards.'

6. 'A moustache is a hive of bacilli.'

7. 'I have no courage to go through that awful stage when a moustache is merely bristles.'

8. 'I wear no moustache because I have a mouth I do not wish to hide. Only men of bad character need wear moustaches.'

9. 'I do not wear a moustache because I do not wish to appear a coward. The mouth is a truer index to character than the eyes, and men can hide emotion behind a moustache. I prefer to be able to control my lips and expression.'

10. 'I do not wear a moustache because my moustache would, when grown, have a green tomato shade. Also, I do not want to look old.'

> **THE 20TH CENTURY**

10 MAMMALS WHICH BECAME EXTINCT IN THE 20TH CENTURY

1. **GILBERT'S POTOROO** (Western Australia, 1900).
2. **PIG-FOOTED BANDICOOT** (South Australia, 1907).
3. **BURCHELL'S ZEBRA** (South Africa, 1910).
4. **NEWFOUNDLAND WHITE WOLF** (Newfoundland, c. 1911).
5. **BARBARY LION** (North Africa, c. 1922).
6. **BUBAL HARTEBEEST** (Algeria, 1923).
7. **SYRIAN ONAGER** (Middle East, 1930).
8. **SCHOMBURGK'S DEER** (Thailand, 1932).
9. **BALI TIGER** (Bali, 1937).
10. **CARIBBEAN MONK SEAL** (Caribbean, 1952).

When martyrs were thrown to the lions in Roman times, it was to a huge Barbary lion, a creature whose mane covered almost half of its body. But then the Arabs hunted them, encouraged by governments which allowed any tribes that killed the lions to be exempt from taxation. The creature's last stronghold was in the Great Atlas Mountains and it was there that the last true Barbary lion was killed in 1922, although attempts have subsequently been made to reconstruct the species in zoos. Other creatures hunted to extinction include the Newfoundland white wolf, whose demise was the direct result of the Newfoundland government having set a bounty on wolves back in 1842, and Schomburgk's deer, a mysterious creature never seen in the wild by a European. It was hunted for its antlers which were said to contain magical and medicinal properties and were used in the lucrative Chinese pharmaceutical trade.

> THE 20TH CENTURY

10 BIRDS WHICH BECAME EXTINCT IN THE 20TH CENTURY

1. BLACK MAMO (Hawaii, 1907).
2. HUIA (New Zealand, 1907).
3. SLENDER-BILLED GRACKLE (Mexico, 1910).
4. GUADELOUPE STORM-PETREL (West Indies, 1912).
5. CAROLINA PARAKEET (U.S.A., 1914).
6. PASSENGER PIGEON (U.S.A., 1914).
7. NORFOLK ISLAND STARLING (Australia, 1925).
8. GRAND CAYMAN THRUSH (West Indies, 1938).
9. NEW ZEALAND BUSH WREN (New Zealand, 1972).
10. COLOMBIAN GREBE (South America, 1977).

The Guadeloupe storm-petrel was wiped out by partly by imported domestic cats, while the loss of the huia was a particular blow since it was the only species in which the male and female had radically different-shaped beaks. But the most startling decline was undoubtedly that of the passenger pigeon. In 1810, it was just about the commonest bird in the world. A total of 2,230,272,000 passenger pigeons were estimated in a single flock and these huge gatherings used to darken the skies and break off hefty branches from trees, so great were their numbers. Yet a century later, the bird was extinct, its downfall hastened by American Indians who lit fires in the bird's breeding areas. In 1909, a reward of $1,500 was offered for information on a nesting pair but all claims proved to be false, the majority turning out to be mourning doves. Five years later, the last passenger pigeon died in captivity in the Cincinnati Zoological Gardens.

> THE 20TH CENTURY

20 NEW MAMMALS DISCOVERED IN THE 20TH CENTURY

1. **OKAPI** (Zaire, 1901).
2. **ROTHSCHILD'S GIRAFFE** (Uganda, 1901).
3. **MOUNTAIN GORILLA** (Zaire, 1902).
4. **SEA MINK** (U.S.A., 1903).
5. **PACARANA** (Ethiopia, 1904) — also known as 'the terrible mouse'.
6. **MOUNTAIN NYALA** (Ethiopia, 1910) — an antelope.
7. **HERO SHREW** (Uganda, 1910).
8. **PYGMY HIPPOPOTAMUS** (Liberia, 1913).
9. **SCALY-TAILED POSSUM** (Australia, 1917).
10. **LONGMAN'S BEAKED WHALE** (Australia, 1926).
11. **PYGMY CHIMPANZEE** (Zaire, 1928).
12. **KOUPREY** (Cambodia, 1937) — an ox-like creature.
13. **SELEVIN'S DORMOUSE** (Kazakhstan, 1938).
14. **BLACK-SHOULDERED OPOSSUM** (South America, 1950).
15. **GOLDEN LANGUR** (India, 1955) — a species of monkey.
16. **COCHITO** (Gulf of California, 1958) — a small porpoise.
17. **RED GORAL** (Southern Asia, 1964) — a goat-like relative of the antelope family.
18. **CHACOAN PECCARY** (South America, 1974) — a pig-like animal.
19. **GOLDEN-CROWNED SIFAKA** (Madagascar, 1989) — a species of lemur.
20. **BLACK-FACED LION TAMARIN** (Brazil, 1992) — a small monkey.

With its spine of bony knobs to prevent it from being crushed by rocks when burrowing, the little hero shrew can withstand tremendous weights. It is said that its backbone can bear the weight of a 12-stone human. The poor sea mink was scientifically recognized in 1903...but only after it had become extinct. The last one was found dead around 1880 near Jonesport, Maine.

> **THE 20TH CENTURY**

20 NEW BIRDS DISCOVERED IN THE 20TH CENTURY

1. FEARFUL OWL (Solomon Islands, 1901).
2. ROTHSCHILD'S PEACOCK PHEASANT (Borneo, 1902).
3. WAKE ISLAND RAIL (Wake Island, Pacific, 1903).
4. RUFOUS-HEADED ROBIN (China, 1905).
5. MIKADO PHEASANT (Taiwan, 1906).
6. NDUK EAGLE OWL (Tanzania, 1906).
7. AFRICAN BROADBILL (Zaire, 1908).
8. ROTHSCHILD'S MYNAH (Bali, 1911).
9. CRESTED SHELDUCK (Korea, 1913).
10. IMPERIAL PHEASANT (Vietnam, 1924).
11. BAKER'S REGENT BOWERBIRD (New Guinea, 1928).
12. RIBBON-TAILED BIRD OF PARADISE (New Guinea, 1938).
13. ARCHBOLD'S BOWERBIRD (New Guinea, 1939).
14. AFRICAN BAY OWL (Zaire, 1951).
15. SOKOKE SCOPS OWL (Kenya, 1965).
16. ALDABRAN WARBLER (Seychelles, 1968).
17. LONG-WHISKERED OWLET (Peru, 1976).
18. AMSTERDAM ALBATROSS (Amsterdam Island, Indian Ocean, 1978).
19. AMAZONIAN PARROTLET (Peru, 1985).
20. EL ORO PARAKEET (Ecuador, 1985).

Discovered in 1903, the Wake Island rail was extinct by 1946. It was wiped out when the island was occupied by Japanese soldiers during World War Two. With food supplies scarce, they found a tasty local delicacy in the rail and proceeded to eat every last bird.

> **THE 20TH CENTURY**

10 MISS WORLD WINNERS OF THE 1960S

1. **NORMA CAPPEGLI (Argentina, 1960).**

2. **ROSEMARIE FRANKLAND (U.K., 1961).**

3. **RINA LODDERS (Holland, 1962).**

4. **CAROLE CRAWFORD (Jamaica, 1963).**

5. **ANN SIDNEY (U.K., 1964).**

6. **LESLEY LANGLEY (U.K., 1965).**

7. **REITA FARIA (India, 1966).**

8. **MADELEINE HARTOG-BEL (Peru, 1967).**

9. **PENNY PLUMMER (Australia, 1968).**

10. **EVA RUEBER-STAIER (Austria, 1969).**

The most famous Miss World of the 1960s was probably Reita Faria, the first Indian woman to wear a swimsuit in a beauty contest. And instead of wanting to travel, meet people and help old ladies across the road, she declared that her ambition was to be a gynaecologist.

> THE 20TH CENTURY

10 WORLD WAR TWO ADVERTISING AND PROPAGANDA SLOGANS

1. HITLER WILL SEND NO WARNING — SO ALWAYS CARRY YOUR GAS MASK.

2. DIG FOR VICTORY.

3. FOR A HEALTHY, HAPPY JOB, JOIN THE WOMEN'S LAND ARMY.

4. MOTHERS — SEND THEM OUT OF LONDON: GIVE THEM A CHANCE OF GREATER SAFETY AND HEALTH. (Government encouragement for parents to have their children evacuated).

5. MAKE DO AND MEND. (Handy hints from the Board of Trade to help women extend the life of clothes by renovating old items).

6. IS YOUR JOURNEY REALLY NECESSARY? (Railway posters urging passengers to think twice before travelling on busy lines).

> **THE 20TH CENTURY**

7. KEEP A PIG. (Part of the push for self-sufficiency, pigs providing food).

8. CARELESS TALK COSTS LIVES.

9. PLOUGH NOW! BY DAY AND NIGHT. (Ministry of Agriculture advice to maintain food supplies).

10. UP HOUSEWIVES AND AT 'EM! (The Ministry of Supply urging women to put paper, metal and even bones out by their dustbin for collection as part of the war effort).

Another treasured wartime slogan was: 'Carrots Keep You Healthy and Help You To See in the Blackout.' As part of its nutrition campaign, the Ministry of Food created two cartoon characters, Dr. Carrot and Potato Pete, who helped promote the benefits of vegetables, especially the theory that carrots helped you see in the dark. The Ministry even insisted that top RAF night-fighter pilots lived on a diet of carrots, and it was not until the end of the war that it emerged that what really helped them shoot down enemy planes was not carrots but the secret new device — radar.

> THE 20TH CENTURY

20 CODENAMES FROM WORLD WAR TWO

1. ATTILA. The German plan for occupying Vichy France following increasing French support for the Allies. The mission was undertaken in November 1942 and resulted in the scuttling of French warships at Toulon.

2. BINGO. A series of U.S. bomber attacks launched in November 1944 on electricity-producing plants supplying the railway system over the Brenner Pass. The aim was to block the main reinforcement route for German forces in Italy.

3. BRISK. The British plan to take the Azores (1940–41) in order to establish air and naval bases there and thus close the 'Atlantic gap' where German U-boats had been able to operate without fear of attack.

4. BUCCANEER. The British scheme to recapture the Andaman Islands in the Bay of Bengal during the spring of 1944. However, a lack of landing craft prevented it from being implemented.

5. BULLDOZER. The aborted British amphibious assault on Akyab, Burma, in the spring of 1944.

6. CROMWELL. The British codeword to be used to signal any German invasion of Britain.

7. CROSSBOW. The 1943–44 British intelligence and photo-reconnaissance campaign to learn about the development, and halt production, of German secret weapons at Peenemünde.

8. FLOWER. A British low-level night intruder mission by de Havilland Mosquito aircraft over German airfields (1944–45).

9. HELLHOUND. The Allied plan for the bombing of Hitler's retreat at Berchtesgaden in the Alps in spring 1945.

> THE 20TH CENTURY

10. **HORLICKS.** The American capture of Biak Island off the North-West coast of New Guinea in the summer of 1944. The exercise saw 5,093 Japanese and 524 Americans killed.

11. **HURRICANE I.** The Allied plan for a bombing offensive against targets in Germany's industrial Ruhr, 1944–45.

12. **IMPERATOR.** The British scheme to seize Boulogne (or a similar French coastal town) via an amphibious assault in the summer of 1942, the aim being to draw German troops from the Eastern front.

13. **KREUZOTTER (viper).** A German operation against Greek resistance forces.

14. **MAGNET.** The Allied exercise of 1942 to move U.S. ground forces into Northern Ireland in readiness for active service in Europe.

15. **MUSTANG.** The Allied contingency plan for a swift overland advance to Naples in the summer of 1943 in case of an Italian collapse after the Sicilian campaign.

16. **PUMPKIN.** The unsuccessful mission by the 17th Indian Light Division in central Burma in December 1943 to wreck the anticipated Japanese offensive.

17. **SHRAPNEL.** The British plan for the seizure of the Cape Verde Islands in spring 1941.

18. **STRANGLE.** An Allied air offensive in spring 1944, the aim of which was to cut all sea, rail and road communication to German troops south of Rome. Although some 20,000 tons of bombs were dropped on railway yards, bridges and tunnels, the operation was only a limited success.

19. **TRUNCHEON.** The 1941 British plan for a landing at Livorno in north-west Italy.

20. **WINDOW.** The release of tin foil strips by British bombers from August 1943. Dropped in bundles, the strips dispersed in mid-air to produce millions of echoes on German radar screens. Since these swamped the echoes produced by the bombers themselves, they served to protect the Allied aircraft.

> **THE 20TH CENTURY**

10 CURE-ALLS OF THE 20TH CENTURY

1. BILE BEANS — 'conquers disorders of the liver, stomach and bowels: a wonderful medicine that copies nature.'

2. BLAIR'S GOUT AND RHEUMATIC PILLS — 'the Great British Remedy'.

3. BUNTER'S NERVINE — 'the best remedy for toothache'.

4. CONGREVE'S ELIXIR — 'cures consumption, asthma, bronchitis, coughs'.

5. 'Fat folk should take FELL'S REDUCING TABLETS — guaranteed to reduce weight a pound a day'.

6. LLEWELLYN'S CUTICLE FLUID.

7. LOCKYER'S HAIR RESTORER.

8. DR. MACKENZIE'S SMELLING BOTTLE — 'for colds, influenza, catarrh etc'.

9. PHOSFERINE — 'the Remedy of Kings: supplied by Royal Command to the King of Greece, the Queen of Romania and the Empress of Russia.'

10. RANKIN'S HEAD OINTMENT — 'kills all nits and vermin'.

Even Marmite was once viewed as having remedial powers for a wide range of diseases. In the early 1950s, a special booklet was produced by the medical profession extolling the virtues of Marmite. Its high Vitamin B content meant that it was considered efficacious for those with diabetes, gastric ulcers and rheumatism as well as nervous and mental complaints. It was prescribed in the Eastern tropics where burning feet and beriberi were prevalent while the Medical Research Council's 1951 report on Deficiency Diseases in Japanese Prison Camps stated that Marmite yeast extract had proved effective in the treatment of scrotal dermatitis. The patients were presumably the original 'Marmite soldiers'...

> THE 20TH CENTURY

10 PRODUCTS OF THE 20TH CENTURY NAMED AFTER THEIR INVENTOR

1. **ADIDAS SHOES** (German shoemaker Adolf 'Adi' Dassler).
2. **ALMAY** (American chemist and his wife, Al and May Schieffelin).
3. **BERLEI** (Australian businessman Fred Burley).
4. **BIC** (French inventor Marcel Bich).
5. **BIRDS EYE** (American businessman Clarence Birdseye).
6. **COTY** (Corsican-born industrialist François Coty).
7. **HARPIC** (London sanitary engineer Harry Pickup).
8. **KENWOOD CHEF** (British entrepreneur Ken Wood).
9. **MARS BAR** (American sweet manufacturer Forrest E. Mars).
10. **RAWLPLUG** (London building contractor John J. Rawlings).

A minor maintenance problem at the British Museum led to the invention of the humble Rawlplug in 1919. The museum needed electrical fittings to be fixed to the walls unobtrusively and without damaging the masonry but this was not easy using the traditional method of chiselling a hole, plugging it with wood and then screwing the fitting into the wood. Fortunately, Kensington builder John J. Rawlings solved the problem by inventing a fibre plug, made of jute bonded with animal blood. He called it the Rawlplug. Perrier Water was named after the inventor's doctor. Recuperating after a serious motor accident, Englishman St. John Harmsworth, brother of newspaper magnates Lord Northcliffe and Lord Rothermere, visited the French spa town of Vergeze in 1903. There he was introduced by his doctor, Louis Perrier, to the local spring, Les Bouillons. Harmsworth decided to market the bubbling water and named it after Dr. Perrier, moulding the famous green bottles on the Indian clubs he had been using to strengthen his arms and back following the car accident.

> **THE 20TH CENTURY**

10 INNOVATIONS OF THE 20TH CENTURY WHICH WERE INITIALLY REJECTED

1. BARBIE DOLL. A number of toy buyers wouldn't touch Barbie when she made her debut in 1959, considering her to be too adult. Barbie's creator, Ruth Handler, later admitted: 'The toy buyers didn't care for Barbie at first. And many of them did not order the doll. They did not think mothers would buy a doll with breasts.'

2. CORRECTION FLUID. The brainchild of Bette Nesmith Graham, mother of former Monkee Michael Nesmith, correction fluid was offered to IBM in 1956 under the brand name 'Mistake Out'. When they rejected it, Bette changed the name to 'Liquid Paper' and set up her own cottage industry, using the family kitchen as a laboratory and the garage as a bottling plant. By the end of 1957, she was settling 100 bottles of liquid paper a month.

3. FOLD-UP BICYCLE. Alex Moulton of Bradford-on-Avon, Wiltshire, designed the revolutionary folding bicycle in 1958 and offered it to Raleigh the following year. They rejected it, maintaining that the public would never take to such an unusual machine. Moulton pressed on and by 1965, sales had reached 70,000. In 1967, Raleigh bought Moulton out.

4. HOVERCRAFT. By the late 1950s, Christopher Cockerell had perfected the idea of the hovercraft and tried to sell his idea to industry. But aircraft companies showed little interest because it wasn't an aircraft and shipping firms rejected it because it wasn't a boat. The concept went nowhere for a year until, in 1958, Cockerell finally received the backing and financial support of the National Research Development Corporation.

> **THE 20TH CENTURY**

5. MONOPOLY. Conceived by unemployed Philadelphia heating engineer Clarence B. Darrow, Monopoly was turned down flat by games manufacturers Parker Bros. Convinced they were wrong, Darrow had 5,000 copies made up by a local manufacturer and met with such success that in 1935 Parker Bros. took over production after all.

6. PHOTOCOPIER. Oklahoma office worker George C. Beidler thought up the world's first photocopier back in 1903 but, because it was painfully slow, it attracted minimal attention. Then in 1938, American patent lawyer Chester Carlson improved upon the invention but he too struggled to find a research institute interested in developing his idea. It was not until 1959, 57 years after Beidler's dream of an office copier, that the first automatic photocopier, the Xerox 914, came on to the market.

7. SAFETY RAZOR. The invention of King Camp Gillette, the safety razor went on sale in 1903 after years of teething trouble. But just 51 razors were sold throughout the USA. The following year, Gillette sold 90,000.

8. TRIVIAL PURSUIT. Formulated in 1982 by three young Canadians — Chris Haney, Scott Abbott John Haney — Trivial Pursuit took 45 minutes to conceive but four years to market. They lost $45,000 on the first batch, to the dismay of 18-year-old unemployed artist Michael Wurstlin who had designed both board and logo in return for five shares in the company. By 1986, the shares were worth $500,000 each.

9. TUPPERWARE. When Earl Silas Tupper first marketed his new product in 1945, he boasted about its unique, water-tight, air-tight seal. However, the seal very nearly proved his downfall since demonstrators at retail stores were unable to operate it.

10. VACUUM CLEANER. In 1902 Hubert Cecil Booth formed the Vacuum Cleaner Company Ltd. but, rather than sell his new invention, he chose to provide a service to the public. The huge apparatus arrived at a customer's house on a horse-drawn van and was parked outside while long hoses were threaded through the windows to suck up the dust.

> THE 20TH CENTURY

10 INVENTIONS OF THE 20TH CENTURY WHICH ARE STILL SEARCHING FOR A MARKET

1. In February 1994, BRYAN PATRIE from Menlo Park, near San Francisco, patented the Watercolour Intelligent Nightlight, a device which reminds men to lower the lavatory seat when they have finished. Nicknamed 'the marriage saver', it only works in the dark when men are apparently at their laziest. If the seat is left up, an infra-red beam reflects back off the seat and switches on a red warning light, shaming the man into action. If the seat is down, a green light glows. During research, one half-asleep tester, seeing the red beam in the bowl, thought it was blood and that he was dying.

2. Travelling on Philadelphia public transport, MRS. NATALIE STOLP had noticed how 'flirtatious young men' deliberately used the crowded conditions as an excuse to press a knee or thigh against their feminine neighbour. Her 1914 patent sought to stem the rising sap by attaching a spring to the lady's underskirt which responded to pressure by releasing a short, sharp point into the offender's flesh.

3. In the 1980s, three French women — DOMINIQUE PEIGNOUX, YVETTE GUYS and FRANÇOISE DEKAN — marketed a musical nappy whereby a contraption was tucked inside a baby's nappy and played "When the Saints Go Marching In" as soon as it became wet.

4. In 1919, JOHN HUMPHREY of Connecticut invented an unusual alarm

> THE 20TH CENTURY

clock: one which would rouse someone from his slumbers by hitting him. The apparatus consisted of a timepiece attached to an adjustable rod with a rubber ball on the end. When the alarm on the clock went off, instead of a bell ringing, the rod would be activated, causing the ball to hit the desired area of the sleeper's anatomy. Humphrey deemed his device to be of great benefit to deaf people or invalids who might be upset by bells...but who presumably didn't mind being whacked over the head with a ball.

5. Helium-filled furniture was the brainchild of WILLIAM A. CALDERWOOD of Peoria, Arizona. His 1989 patent envisaged furniture floating to the ceiling when not in use, thereby allowing extra floor space. When required, the furniture would be pulled back down to the floor by a rope.

6. EARL M. CHRISTOPHERSON of Seattle patented a 1960 device to enable people to look inside their own ears.

7. THOMAS FERRY of Wilmington, Delaware, perfected a moustache-guard in 1901. He said it was 'designed to hold the mustache away from the lips and to prevent the lodgement of food thereon while eating'. It consisted of a number of upward-pointing teeth inserted through the moustache from below 'to support the long flowing ends of the mustache which otherwise might droop down in the way'. An elastic tape was then strapped around the lip hair.

8. In 1984, Welshpool publican PHIL LEWIS was discussing potato crisp flavours with some Romany customers. They told him of an old gypsy delicacy — hedgehog baked in clay — and suggested the possibility of hedgehog-flavoured crisps. Using a closely-guarded recipe, Lewis set to work in his kitchen to produce the first packets. Customers likened the taste to smokey

THE 20TH CENTURY

bacon but, as the venture attracted more and more publicity, animal-lovers protested and Lewis was forced to abandon the snack for more traditional flavours. Bensons Crisps bought him out in 1988 and kept Hedgehog on as a brand name rather than a flavour.

9. It was in 1966 that America's THOMAS J. BAYARD invented a vibrating toilet seat, acting on the belief that physical stimulation of the buttocks is effective in relieving constipation.

10. To reduce pedestrian casualties in 1960, DAVID GUTMAN from Philadelphia came up with a special pedestrian bumper designed to be fixed to the front of a car. Not only would it cushion the impact in the event of a collision but it also had a huge pair of claws which would grab the pedestrian around the waist to prevent him dropping to the tarmac.

ALSO AVAILABLE IN ALL GOOD BOOKS STORES: